Praise for Lynn Andrews

"Lynn Andrews continues to write of her apprenticeship to the Native American shaman Agnes Whistling Elk in this companion to her earlier *Medicine Woman*. The most remarkable element of this book is its ability to communicate a sense of both the physical and spiritual lessons that Andrews has learned during her stays with the Cree Indians.

"Her previous book detailed her initiation into the teachings of the Sisterhood of the Shields, a secret society traditionally the sole province of Native American women, and in this account she continues her education, revealing in the process why she felt compelled to return to Whistling Elk for further study.

"Both books are notable not only for the glimpse they provide of an unfamiliar culture, but also for Andrews's quietly powerful style and the humility with which she opens herself to new and often seemingly alien experiences."

—*Booklist* (American Library Association)

"We are lucky that the likes of Agnes Whistling Elk still exist, and that one such as Lynn Andrews has had the opportunity to experience the ways of a medicine woman and has lived to write about it. Andrews's books are a glimpse into a world of the miraculous and the eternal, and intimate a true understanding of the extraordinary laws of nature."

—*Yoga Journal*

"A beautiful study of an unfamiliar culture . . . excellent reading."
—*The McCor*

D1501604

Spirit Woman

Spirit Woman

THE TEACHINGS OF THE SHIELDS

Lynn Andrews

ILLUSTRATIONS BY N. SCOTT MOMADAY

Previously published as *Flight of the Seventh Moon*

JEREMY P. TARCHER/PUTNAM
a member of Penguin Putnam Inc.
New York

Most Tarcher/Putnam books are available at special quantity discounts for
bulk purchase for sales promotions, premiums, fund-raising, and educational needs.
Special books or book excerpts also can be created to fit specific needs. For details,
write Putnam Special Markets, 375 Hudson Street, New York, NY 10014.

Jeremy P. Tarcher/Putnam
a member of
Penguin Putnam Inc.
375 Hudson Street
New York, NY 10014
www.penguinputnam.com
First published as *Flight of the Seventh Moon* in 1984 by Harper & Row, Publishers

First Jeremy P. Tarcher/Putnam Edition 2002

Acknowledgment is made for permission to reprint the following:
From Hilda Doolittle, *Collected Poems of H. D.*, copyright © 1957 by Norman Holmes
Pearson; reprinted by permission of New Directions Publishing Corporation, agents.
From *News of the Universe*, chosen and introduced by Robert Bly,
copyright © 1980 by Robert Bly; reprinted by permission of Sierra Club Books.
From Philip Lamantia, *Becoming Visible*, copyright © 1981 by Philip Lamantia;
reprinted by permission of City Lights Books.
From Howard A. Norman, *The Wishing Bone Cycle*, copyright © 1982
by Howard A. Norman, reprinted by permission of Ross-Erickson, Inc., Publishers.
From Ursula K. LeGuin, *Hard Words and Other Poems*, copyright © 1977
by Ursula K. LeGuin; reprinted by permission of Harper & Row, Publishers, Inc.
"The Moon By Arrangement," from *Thread the Silence Like a Needle*
by Jack Crimmins, copyright © 1983 by Jack Crimmins; reprinted by
permission of Maya Press, Los Angeles.

Library of Congress Cataloging-in-Publication Data
Andrews, Lynn V.
[Flight of the seventh moon]
Spirit woman : the teachings of the shields / Lynn Andrews.—
1st Jeremy P. Tarcher/Putnam pbk. ed.
p.   cm.
Originally published: Flight of the seventh moon.
San Francisco : Harper & Row, © 1984.
ISBN 1-58542-170-7
I. Title
BP610.A54143   2002   2002018865
299'.7—dc21

Book design by Jim Mennick
Printed in the United States of America
1 3 5 7 9 10 8 6 4 2

This book is dedicated to my mother Rosalyn and my daughter Vanessa whose love and understanding have made my journey possible.

With special appreciation to Twila Nitsch Yehwehnode of the Seneca Nation and Paula Gunn Allen for being the medicine women that they are.

With great thanks to John V. Loudon, my editor, whose thoughtfulness and dedication have helped me tremendously.

Contents

THE MOON IN YOUR HANDS

If you take the moon in your hands
and turn it round
(heavy, slightly tarnished platter)
you're there;

if you pull dry sea-weed from the sand
and turn it round
and wonder at the underside's bright amber,
your eyes

look out as they did here,
(you don't remember)
when my soul turned round,

perceiving the other-side of everything,
mullein-leaf, dogwood leaf, moth-wing
and dandelion-seed under the ground.

—H.D. [HILDA DOOLITTLE],
from *The Selected Poems of H. D.*

Preface

This is a true story. Some of the names and places in this book have been changed to protect the privacy of those involved.

I am a woman.

The last several years of my life have been spent on a spiritual quest. My path led me first to many male teachers. Each of them, in their own way, gave me startling insights into my own nature. Still, something was lacking. I knew I wanted to learn from a woman—for me, that was the only way. I was lucky. After a series of extraordinary events, Agnes Whistling Elk, a Native American Medicine Woman living in Manitoba, Canada, became my teacher.

When I first met Agnes, I asked her if she thought it was strange for someone from Beverly Hills to be sitting in her quiet cabin in Manitoba asking for help.

"There are always helpers and signs to point the way for anyone who is willing to follow them," she said. "Unknowingly, for the first time in your life, you have followed your true path. No, it is not surprising that you are here. Many omens have spoken of your coming, and I would be surprised if it were any other way. You know that enlightenment is arrived at in a different way for a woman than for a man."

I asked Agnes if she taught men the same as woman. She laughed and said I should discover that answer for myself. "Teach the next ten men you meet how to have a baby."

Spirit Woman (previously published as *Flight of the Seventh Moon*) describes how Agnes initiated me into my womanliness and selfhood. Through a series of visions and ceremonies, she took me around a circle of learning, and gave me a working mandala, a shield that I can carry in my everyday life. Within the experiences of my rite of passage is the ancient wisdom of woman. My story is like the story of all women involved in search. Our situations are different because we all are unique, but our source of understanding is the same.

Agnes has never told me what I must learn. She has simply put me into situations where I must grow and change to survive. *Medicine Woman* tells of how Agnes guided me through the four aspects of my beginning work. Much of this involved making me physically strong, because she feels that there must be a balance between spiritual learning and physical endurance. Agnes also placed me in situations where I learned to balance the male and female elements within me. Much of that training had to do with the search for the sacred marriage basket. Finally, she taught me about making an act of power or an act of beauty in the world. For me that was writing a book. I learned that the reason for an act of beauty is to create a mirror for yourself so that you can begin to know intimately who you are. Agnes also made it very clear to me through paranormal events, my travels to Canada, and the work in dreaming, that it is very important for us to be lifted out of our mechanical existence so that real change—perhaps even transformation—has a chance to occur. Our structures and beliefs must be suspended so that something new can be heard.

I once asked Agnes what she thought about the biblical expression, "many are called but few are chosen." She laughed and said that we are all called and we all are chosen if we simply have the courage to step into the unknown. I have written so that you may also share in the ancient traditions as memorized by Agnes Whistling Elk and the Sisterhood of the Shields.

The Sisterhood of the Shields is a secret society based in the ancient traditions of woman. Although its membership has long been limited to Native Americans, the energy changes on our planet have made it necessary to initiate women of other races. We share our knowledge collectively, between tribes and nations, in an attempt to bring balance, wisdom, and a more complete view of truth to the land.

Spirit Woman

Protector-of-Children Shield: South

Sometimes I go about pitying myself,
and all the time
I am being carried on great winds across the sky.
                    —OJIBWAY, adapted by Robert Bly
            from the translation of Frances Densmore

I stood at the entrance to the Beverly Hills Hotel. The warm wind
from the south rippled like clean silk on my skin. The air smelled of
honeysuckle and I took a deep breath, trying to relax. I was
nervously waiting for Hyemeyohsts Storm, the author of *Seven
Arrows* and medicine man from Montana, and two film producers
from New York who wanted to make a film based on my book,
Medicine Woman. The thought of seeing Hyemeyohsts again
relieved some of my anxiety. I glanced up at the ominous black
clouds overhead and wondered what could be keeping him so long.

As I waited for the valet to take my car, I gazed at the hotel's
sixteen-acre parkland. The pool, cabanas, and fabulous guests—kings
and queens, movie stars, business executives—made the hotel very
special, and ordinarily I would have been happy to be here. But
today was different. I was on my way to Canada to stay with Agnes
Whistling Elk, the Cree Indian woman who had become my
teacher. I had rented my home a few days early, and planned to stay
at the hotel in the interim.

As the valet took my car and bags, I was distracted by the arrival
of a flesh pink Cadillac Seville, from which a gorgeous girl emerged.

All eyes were riveted on her, and no wonder—her outfit was flesh pink, and so was her tea-cup poodle. That's Hollywood, I thought ruefully. A limousine with license plates that read "FATHER" had also pulled up to the hotel, but with much less fanfare. As I watched from behind a tall pillar covered with ivy and flowers, all the doors to the limousine suddenly burst open at once, as if they had a mind of their own. No one got out for a moment, and then there was a flurry of activity as uniformed attendants scrambled to help an elderly gentleman out of the back seat and into a waiting electric wheel chair. I didn't recognize him, but he seemed somehow familiar. He had a distinctive way of lifting his gnarled hand and impatiently directing everyone. He was almost growling at his embarrassed young chauffeur, who tripped and nearly fell over the wheelchair as he lifted it up over the curb.

As the distinguished gray-haired gentleman rolled past me, he suddenly swerved, brushing my leg and sending me tumbling toward the flower bed. I could hear the pansies being crushed beneath my high heels and I swung my arms around wildly, trying to keep my balance.

A hand grabbed my elbow. It was Hyemeyohsts, who had rushed up just in time to steady me. I lifted my foot out of the newly watered garden and removed my mud-covered high heel. One shoe on and one off, I hobbled my way into the hotel lobby with Storm, where I excused myself and went into the powder room. As I stood in front of the sink wiping the dirt off my high heel, I caught the reflection of a medium-tall blonde woman in a white silk dress staring at me from the mirror. I hesitated, peering at her image. She kept going in and out of focus. With a start, I realized I was looking at myself. My head ached.

I sat down on a pink velvet stool in front of the mirror and tried to clear my vision. Waves of nausea passed through me. I shook my head and watched the unfamiliar blurred image in the mirror. I looked awful and felt even worse. I felt like a patient coming out of anesthesia, who wakes to see unfamiliar walls and feels frightened and helpless. I wished Agnes could tell me what to do.

Agnes Whistling Elk is my teacher. This Native American

medicine woman has many truly formidable qualities. She is old, yet often appears young and agile. For several years she has been dedicated to teaching me how to use the ancient wisdom of woman.

Agnes is often assisted by a medicine woman named Ruby Plenty Chiefs. Ruby is more gruff and often times rude. She makes me feel unsure of myself, and seems to reflect my own inner fears. She seems egotistical. But her powers are also formidable, and her every move has a purpose.

My training, as I see it now, had to do with breaking the cultural limitations imposed upon me—and, by inference, imposed on all women. When I told Agnes of my intention to write *Medicine Woman*, she warned me of the struggle I faced:

"You are writing about the ancient power of woman, about a teaching that has been nearly forgotten. There are some people who will fight against your message, but it is so necessary that it be heard that you must try. You are a white woman from a glamorous city, and they will find it hard to believe."

Agnes believes deeply in the need to restore the balance between male and female energy on her beloved mother earth. She feels that we live in a time of vision, a time when the people of the earth are once again ready to hear many secrets that have long been hidden. This a time of cleansing and breaking away. We can destroy our earth mother or learn to live in harmony with her. To learn to live in harmony in this day, both men and women must reeducate their femaleness. Agnes sees that it is the woman in all of us that needs to be healed and reborn.

It was in seeking to recapture this female energy that I encountered my adversary, Red Dog, who had stolen it, in the form of a sacred marriage basket, for himself. He is a white man who sought out Agnes in order to restore the female balance in his own consciousness. But Agnes is a hard taskmaster, and Red Dog was cruel. When he tried to take all the power for himself, Agnes cut him off and he became not a shaman but a sorcerer, who turned toward evil instead of love. I was and am more frightened of Red Dog than of anyone on earth.

My reverie was suddenly broken by a familiar voice. "Lynn, listen to me. You are in grave danger, and something must be done." I heard Agnes's voice so clearly in my head that I looked around for a moment to see if she were there. But there was only a well-dressed young woman washing her hands at the sink and the sound of "Strangers in the Night" on the piped-in Muzak.

"You have no shields, no protection. You are wide open and asking for attack. If you don't want Red Dog to attack you, you must learn to make shields."

"Shields?" I wondered, fear crawling up my spine.

"Yes," she said, answering my thoughts. I closed my eyes. I could almost see her sitting at the wooden table in her cabin, an intense look on her ancient Indian face, her long grey braids brushing her red Pendleton shirt. "You see, your light is growing on the other side and you're attracting all kinds of influences—good and bad—like moths to a flame. What is born into the physical world also exists in the spirit world."

I thought to myself, "What kind of shields?"

Again she answered, "The kind of shield that allows only the thought forms of light to enter and returns all darkness and destruction to the sender." Then she repeated slowly, in a far off voice in my mind. "Back to the shooter. You're in trouble because you stole back the marriage basket and defeated Red Dog. You wouldn't stand in front of a bobcat and ask him to leap on you, would you? You'd protect yourself, wouldn't you? Well, you're in a lot more danger than that! When you achieve a dream, you take that dream to the Spirit House for the Kachinas, the Keepers of the Great Dream, to manifest. So why didn't you ask them for protection?"

"I didn't know I was supposed to," I said, as if I were actually talking to her.

"Protection is always the first thing you ask for." She sounded impatient. "The second thing is direction. I didn't think you were that stupid."

"What do I do, Agnes? Will you help me?" I asked out loud. The woman washing her hands looked at me strangely and left quickly.

Agnes started to laugh. "Lynn, you're playing the part of Poor

Cow again, indulging in your own lack of courage." And then her voice was gone.

I felt exhausted. Was Agnes's voice a delusion? I had been in a trance. How long had I been in the powder room? It seemed like days. I glanced at my watch. Only minutes had passed. I hurried down to the lobby, still feeling quite ill.

"Hey, Lynn, are you okay?" Storm asked, obviously very concerned.

"Yes . . . I feel a little weak, that's all. Probably need something to eat." I must have looked awful, because he grabbed my arm and steered me across the red-carpeted foyer, his eyes never leaving me for an instant.

We sat down in the Polo Lounge and ordered lunch. The first thing I was aware of was the loud volume of voices. I felt again as if I were coming out of a haze. As it cleared, my senses were heightened. The noise level was incredible. I had to blink my eyes against the light that reflected off the highly polished silver on the tables and the expensive jewelry on the patrons. I shook my head to clear it. Hyemeyohsts still held my arm. He reached over gently and took my chin, turning my face towards him. "What's going on with you?" He sounded alarmed.

"Hyemeyohsts, I'm feeling terribly ill." A quick movement from across the room caught my eye. There he was again—that old man in the wheelchair. For a moment, the room seemed too quiet. Two well-dressed men appeared—one older and one younger. I realized they were the two men we had come to meet. "You must be Lynn Andrews," said the younger one.

I was too dizzy to get up, so I extended my hand. "Mr. Stevens, how are you? This is Heyemeyohsts Storm." I smiled thickly. They must have thought I was drunk.

"And may I present our money man from New York—Jack Portland," the older gentleman smiled, and they both sat down. Jack looked at me a long time and then said, "Lynn, I'm going to invest in your film idea, so let's just get that out of the way. I agree to all the terms we discussed on the phone. My lawyer will call your agent tomorrow, okay?"

"Yes."

"What I really want to talk about are your book and your experiences." He settled back in his chair with the customary assuredness of someone who commands attention. He adjusted his protruding abdomen back under his belt, and cocked his head to one side. "About all this stuff concerning sorcery and Red Dog. We all know there is no such thing as sorcery, let alone. . . ." As he spoke, a brilliant shaft of light cut into the room from one of the high garden windows. Flecks of dust in the air made it glow, lighting Jack's grey hair like a halo. Suddenly, images of that incredible confrontation with Red Dog two years earlier came flooding into my mind.

Following Agnes's instructions, I had gone to Red Dog's cabin to steal back the powerful marriage basket. Thinking I was alone, I reached for it. Just then, he appeared out of nowhere. Red Dog had enormous power, and, as he too lunged for the basket, great fibres of light shot out from the basket, connecting him to it. The tricks of light in the Polo Lounge seemed to bring that moment back in full force. Jack shifted in his chair. The light from the window bounced off a spoon and glared into my eyes.

Jack continued, "And what's all this crap about luminous fibres? I'm pretty gullible, but how do you expect me to believe that the sorcerer dissolved into an old man as you cut the last one? That must have been a metaphor, right?"

Now, as I looked at Jack, the shaft of light was behind him once more. I felt it odd and synchronistic that he wanted to discuss those final moments when I stood face to face with the one I most feared.

Suddenly, I was even more nauseated. I tried to breathe deeply, collecting myself with all the energy I possessed. A terrible pressure was building in my head and my vision was blurring. For a moment I could hear the winds of Manitoba blowing through the room of Red Dog's cabin, and I heard the low, ferocious growl of his voice.

"I insist that you admit to us that there is no such thing as sorcery," Jack demanded. I started to double over in my chair with a stomach cramp. The seizure passed unnoticed, and the two men busied themselves ordering hors d'oeuvres and more drinks.

Across the room, I noticed the man in the electric wheelchair, bathed in a pool of light. He was wearing an immaculate and magnificently styled black pin-striped suit. He kept running his fingers slowly through his thick white hair, apparently enjoying the feel of it. His profile was oddly familiar. I squinted at him, wondering what it was that attracted me to him. I saw him run his hands over the wheelchair, and then I looked at his feet and gasped. Hyemeyohsts grabbed me as I started to shudder. The old man was wearing beaded leather mocassins. The cut glass beads were glinting in the sunlight. Slowly, the man turned and looked at me squarely. There was something bestial in his eyes.

"His feet, . . ." I stammered to Hyemeyohsts. "Red Dog." At the pronouncement of this name, I doubled over in pain. I clutched at my legs, and felt something attached to my calf. "Hyemeyohsts . . . my leg . . . on my leg!" Storm bent down, knocking over the remainder of his drink. An old turquoise trade bead was actually embedded in my leg! I frantically tore at it, it fell and skidded across the floor. I heard dark winds howling in my head. I began to cough violently. "I'm choking to death," I managed to say. I could hardly breathe.

"Hey, what's the matter, Lynn?" Jack asked. People were staring at me with pity and contempt. I must have been quite a sight. The maitre d' and Hyemeyohsts assisted me past the curious customers to the elevator. The two producers just sat there, helpless. As the elevator rose, I could feel myself sinking. I remember seeing the number "16" on my room door, and then the great banana leaves printed on the walls seemed to flutter and blur. I was in a cold sweat as Storm lay me back on my bed and closed the drapes.

"Where is your medicine bundle?" he demanded.

"In that leather bag." I pointed to my pile of bags in the corner of the room. Hyemeyohsts ripped open the zipper and pulled out my red medicine blanket, which I had tied with leather thongs. He deftly unrolled it and brought me my gourd rattle, tearing the feather off the stem. He helped me to a sitting position and handed the feather to me.

"Lynn, now you must eat this eagle feather or you will die. Red

Dog has laid the swirls of death upon you. This feather is the only power I can think of that can save you."

I took the small feather without question and began to chew. It sounded like I was crushing bones. Waves of nausea coursed through me. I was convulsed in pain. I chewed and chewed, determined to hold on to life. The phone kept ringing until Storm took it off the hook. People kept pounding on the door. I heard an ambulance wailing in the distance. What a grotesque way to die, I thought. When the feather was completely swallowed, Hyemeyohsts handed me a glassful of some bitter liquid made from the contents of his pouch. "Drink," he ordered, holding me up in a semi-sitting position. I gagged it down and then I collapsed.

I fell into a thankful sleep. My dreams that night appeared from the most healing part of my being. While I was dreaming, I was aware of being tended by merciful energies in the form of stars. My attention was being focused on a tiny blue-white point of light that existed both within my heart and in space. It had an enchanting quality, and yet I felt it within, as the most powerful part of myself.

I awoke at dawn the next day and sneezed from the stench of stale smoke that permeated the air. The ashtray was filled with cigarette butts. Storm was sitting cross-legged on the floor near my bed, his eyes closed, his breathing even. The ravages of room service lay next to him. I was glad he was there for me. He slowly opened his eyes and smiled with such a tender expression that I started to cry. He got up and sat down on the edge of my bed. He looked pale and exhausted. His eyes conveyed clearly that I had nearly died and that he was grateful for my survival. He stroked my forehead gently.

"Lynn, why didn't you tell me that you had no protection?"

"I assumed I did. Well, actually I hadn't given it much thought."

"Lynn, you have taken the woman power of one of the most powerful sorcerers alive and you haven't given 'much thought' to protecting yourself?" He shook his head ruefully. "You novices in medicine are all the same. You are unaware of the real powers of the world even though you've availed yourself of them." He leaned forward and took my hand firmly. "Don't you know that Red Dog is going to try to kill you? He nearly did succeed." Storm's frustration with my stupidity was mounting. He got up and paced, murmuring something I couldn't make out. Then he whirled around and loudly whispered, "You're as wide open as a parking lot. You aren't even wearing your earring. Look, my friend, you must learn immediately how to shield yourself. Your Agnes is the only one who can help you. She is the only one who can save your life.

"I have some business to attend to, and then I'm going to give her the book about all of us," I said weakly. "In a few days."

"Lynn, you are being given the opportunity to become a medicine person, a person capable of seeing and knowing and piercing through all the layers of illusion. You must be a warrioress. Your growth is a process and you may not cut out any step of the journey. Accept the lessons, harsh as they may seem to you. See how identified you are with approval and disapproval. Stop seeing yourself through everybody else's eyes and use your own. Learn to perceive the world from your original starting point." I remembered my dream of the blue-white star. I recalled the words of my father, who said, "I hope after I'm gone that you find someone who cares enough to lovingly correct you. The whole world waits to be lovingly corrected."

We both sighed in unison. I felt a deep feeling of connection with this man and his words. We were one.

After two days of rest, I left for Manitoba, feeling strong again. I landed at Winnepeg in bright sunshine, rented a car, and began my journey to the reserve. From the town of Crowley, it seemed no time at all before I pulled up to Agnes's cabin. I was excited. I grabbed my book and small suitcase and gathered up the grocery bag filled with cigarettes, white bread, bologna, and other foods I knew she liked. As I approached the cabin, wondering if Agnes would be home, the door burst open and out came Agnes, Ruby, and July, Ruby's apprentice, a beautiful Cree woman in her twenties. They were all laughing and bumping into each other like puppies.

"You're late," Ruby said smiling. "We've been expecting you for hours." Agnes laughed at the surprise on my face. July ran to me and took the groceries. She looked at me quizzically and said, "What took you so long, Lynn?"

I was amazed. "There's no way to get a message to anyone out here. How did you know I was coming?"

"Oh, Red Dog phoned ahead to warn us."

They all laughed and hugged me.

"We're having venison tonight in your honor," Agnes said.

I was touched by their warm welcome. I took a deep breath. It all felt so good. For the first time in months I gave myself permission to relax.

Inside, Agnes handed me a paper cup. "Here's some tea for you." Steam was rising from it. There was a moment of silent expectancy, and then I carefully placed my book in the center of the table and waited for their reactions.

"What's that? Even though I'm blind, I can see that you're really full of yourself," Ruby said sharply, as she pointed at the book. Agnes and July looked from one to the other with shrugs.

"That's the book I wrote," I said proudly. "I brought it to read to you."

"What's it about?" Ruby asked.

"It's about you and Agnes and July and Red Dog and the marriage basket and. . . ." I stopped myself. "It's about all of us!" I was beaming with delight.

"What! You never told me you were going to write a book about me."

Agnes laughed. "Ruby, we don't tell you everything."

Ruby looked affronted. "Agnes, you never told me Lynn was writing a book. Oh, I would never have helped you had I known. I would never have loaned you the Mother Rattle."

"Come off it, Ruby. That was my rattle, anyway," Agnes said.

I became alarmed at the sudden turn of events. "Hey, what's happening? I thought you'd all be really happy about the book."

"Well. . . ." Ruby fingered a scab on her left elbow. "I'd like to hear what you've got to say in your book."

"Ruby, eat some dinner," July said, putting a plate of venison in front of her. "Come on, it'll make you feel better."

"Listen, don't tell me what'll make me feel better." She swatted a fly on the table and angrily stabbed the meat on her plate with her fork. Each time I tried to speak and tell them about my experience with Red Dog, Ruby held up her hand to silence me, as if she knew what I was going to say.

I couldn't believe Ruby's outrageous behavior. She was ruining everything. I regarded her suddenly, not as the powerful medicine woman I had written about, but as a spoiled, petulant child determined to ruin the party.

Agnes sat down to eat. Between bites she poked at the book with her fork. A small piece of fat struck to the front page, staining it. I quickly wiped it off as best I could, but the stain remained. My irritation was mounting. This certainly was not the reception I had expected. I withdrew and pictured myself having a good stiff drink at home with civilized people.

Agnes read my expression. "Come on, Lynn, we'll have a real civilized supper and you read to us from your book." Listlessly, I opened to the first page and began to read. The joy of sharing this event was snuffed out for me. Nevertheless, I read on for two whole chapters without looking up even once. I suppose I would have continued, but Ruby was groaning and moaning, holding her belly. I was thoroughly distracted. She finally let out a long belch. That was it. I slammed the book shut.

"Ruby, what's going on?" I asked, looking at her with undisguised disgust.

She whined, "You didn't make me out to be a very nice person—which I am. People will get the idea that I'm an old hag. I'm quite attractive for a lady of my age, don't you think? Agnes? I'm certainly much more attractive than Lynn made out." Ruby fluffed her hair for the imaginary photographers and tossed her head like a young girl.

"Yes, Ruby, but look at what she did to me," Agnes piped in. "I'm in good shape for my age, too!" Agnes sucked in her gut and strutted around like a proud turkey. I had to laugh in spite of my anger.

"Why are you making fun of me?" I asked.

"The least you could have done is say that we're only middle-aged."

"Yeah," Ruby chimed in.

Why were they doing this? Were they ridiculing my own vanity? I was disturbed by the thought.

"Actually, Lynn, it seems like you're favoring Agnes in your book. It's a good thing you aren't my apprentice. I'd feel downright betrayed. You make us both appear old, mean, and tricky." In fact, that was just the way I was experiencing them at that precise moment. Then, with the tone of a proper little girl, Ruby said coyly, "You know we're just as nice as we can be."

I noticed July tip-toeing out the door, apparently unseen by the two old women. They were both preening themselves and strutting back and forth, wringing their hands in an absurd demonstration interspersed with yells to each other and to me. I sat watching in utter disbelief. My feelings were hurt. I felt totally confused. Suddenly, Ruby stopped her shenanigans and turned to face me. She walked over slowly and scanned me with her hands, holding them about two inches from my body. She closed her eyes.

"Lynn, she said, "you use your body as if it were a rag tied onto the tail of your consciousness."

Agnes joined in her laughter and peered at me with her face contorted, poking and plucking at my clothes. I felt assaulted in every way. Ruby sat down, her attitude changing to one of mock concern.

"I'm sure Agnes, your great teacher, has warned you that you are in extreme danger now."

"Well, yes, sort of, but what do you mean?" I looked at Agnes for an explanation.

"I was going to get around to that." Agnes looked a bit sheepish.

"Get around to what?" I asked impatiently. Anxiety began creeping up my groin into my stomach. I started to ask Agnes about hearing her voice at the hotel. I needed desperately to tell her about my near brush with death.

But Ruby interrupted me every time I tried, and waved her hand for silence. "Ha. Now you're in the greatest danger you've ever been in." She leaned forward and whispered, "And you may not survive!"

Agnes suddenly looked very serious.

Ruby glared at Agnes. "I should never have asked you to help me get back at Red Dog."

"You could never have done it without me," Agnes said.

This was all too much. I couldn't control myself. "I feel like a pawn!" I cried out.

"What's a pawn?" Ruby asked innocently.

"It's a piece on a chessboard that doesn't have much power."

"That's you all right," Ruby acknowledged.

"I'm outraged. You've used me and tricked me. Why?" I felt like I was going to choke.

Agnes quietly sat down, cocked her head, and watched me go through my turmoil.

I finally took a breath. "Agnes, what's happening, what aren't you telling me?" I was exploding from sheer frustration!

"Ho! You've stepped into this circle of power, and what did you think would happen?"

Ruby gruffly shoved back her chair. "Where's July?" She walked around the cabin, and then abruptly said, "I'm leaving," and stomped out. A moment later, she poked her head in the door and said, "See you," and left.

It took me a moment to gather my courage again to ask, "What am I doing wrong? I've done as you told me. I thought that my act of writing this book was a form of protection—revealing some of your teaching—bringing these secrets out of darkness into light." My voice sounded as if it were coming from a deep well.

"You've got to start using your head, Lynn."

"I thought I was, Agnes," I said weakly. "I thought you'd be happy about the book." I felt about five years old. "I thought that's what you had instructed me to do." I was on the verge of crying. Agnes got up and poured some more tea. For a moment, she almost looked tender, and then she walked over and patted me rather hard on the head.

"But I thought the marriage basket was going to fill me up?"

"Nope. It makes you complete in a way. But that's just the

beginning." Agnes sighed. "You're my apprentice. It is law that I must help you. Unfortunately," she grinned at me, "I don't have the knowledge you need at this turn of the road. . . ."

"Oh, that's delightful. Now you tell me."

"Ruby can help you."

"Oh, great. The blind leading the blind." I thought of Ruby's insolence and shivered. "She'll never help me. Can you get her to help me?"

"Nope."

"Why not?" I panicked. "She's your friend!"

"She's not my friend. I've never liked Ruby. She's a medicine woman and I respect her. I respect the work she does. Aside from that, she's the most egotistical old bat I've ever known."

"But she's your best—"

Agnes interrupted me. "I've given away a lot to her. You'd think she'd help me. But when the chips are down, Ruby will really put it to you. I don't like her apprentices much, either. July is all right, but Ben and Drum are. . . ." She made a thumbs down motion. "Ruby's let her power go to her head."

"Ben and Drum? You must be kidding!"

Agnes's face was as serious as could be.

"Agnes, how did they become Ruby's apprentices?"

"Ben and Drum were left without a teacher after you took the marriage basket away from Red Dog."

I was shocked.

Agnes continued. "They first came to me and I ran 'em off because I just don't like men apprentices. For me to teach a man, I have to reverse everything. Got no use for them. But Ruby . . . she's a certain kind of medicine woman that has the kind of power they need.

"I saw them coming up the road one day. They were very nervous and made tobacco offerings to me. They had several good blankets, so I let them come on. Drum gave me the tobacco. I said, 'What is it you want from me?' I had to receive them because that is the law. Drum said, 'We want you to teach us and initiate us into your way.' I said, 'I can look at both of you idiots and tell that my heyoka road,

the teachings of the Sacred Clown, or the Contrary, is not for you.
If you want my advice, you should go to someone else. Maybe
someone down south. Maybe Colorado. But if you want real power,
go and learn from Ruby.' They made quite a fuss when they heard
that suggestion. They wanted me, because you, as my apprentice,
had defeated Red Dog, their teacher. They had been Red Dog's
devoted apprentices until you took back the marriage basket and stole
away his woman power. No, he will not be the same until he has
regained his balance. And that will take a long time. Maybe age will
get him."

"Agnes, why do you use the term *heyoka*—isn't that a Lakota
word?"

"I use the word *heyoka* because my teacher was part Cree, part
northern Cheyenne, and part Lakota, and her teacher was Lakota. I
traveled a long way from home to learn from her; it was a long time
ago. I speak many Indian languages and Lakota is one. I learned the
heyoka way in her tongue. She was the only one who could help
me when my daughter went to join the ancestors. I was in great
pain then. I understood very little. Because I learned much from my
Lakota and Cheyenne grandmothers about medicine, I use many of
their words in my work, as does Ruby. Their language has great
power and dignity for me."

"I like the sound of it, too."

"I know you do. I can see that it affects you deeply. It should,
you once spoke Lakota."

"What do you mean?"

"I can't tell you. You need to remember on your own. It will
mean much more to you. But the language sound will take you
back to that place of forgetting and remembering, to a happy life
you once had on the plains long before the white man came."

I bit my lip. Agnes's soft voice and words made me suddenly want
to cry. I looked away. Agnes took my chin in her hand and turned
my face toward her. She made me look at her.

"Oh, I can see you laugh, but I can't watch you cry?" Tears
rolled down my cheeks and she held me for a moment.

Agnes studied my face. She continued, this new, gruff attitude returning. She picked up her teacup and placed it on the very edge of the table. "To get back to what I was saying, I would teach you anything and everything I know, but your needs have put me in a funny position." She flicked her paper teacup off the edge of the table. It fell soundlessly on the floor. Agnes leaned forward. "Ruby and I have always drawn from each other as worthy opponents. Now we'd better all be careful. That lady is capable of anything. Particularly if you really need something from her."

Agnes paused for a moment, and then in a very confidential voice she said, "Actually, I never really thought that Ruby was blind. You certainly wouldn't know it by watching her. I think she just says that to get people to do things for her. You should see how Ben and Drum wait on her. Oh boy, July is very jealous. Anytime anyone makes any demand on Ruby's time, July has a tantrum. I fully expect Ruby to dump all those appentices any day now. They pull on her. But you have to learn from her, whether you like it or not. I don't envy you one bit, Lynn. If you're going to get what you need, you'd better hurry before Ruby dumps the whole lot and disappears. I've heard she has a boyfriend somewhere. She was married once, you know, and she's always thought about going back to that old crank."

"Married? Ruby? And she's not blind? I don't know what you're saying, Agnes. Are you trying to teach me something?"

Agnes laughed. "Yes, of course. I don't want to have anything to do with Ruby. I don't need anything from her. But you do."

"But Agnes, you and Ruby . . . you two are really close."

"It just seemed that way. But I see that your very life depends on her now. If you don't get Ruby to help you, your life isn't worth a plug nickel. But then you wasichus are never taught the need for protection as a child."

I shook my head, feeling small and ashamed of my stupidity. "What do I do, Agnes?"

Agnes shrugged, "I suppose we'll think of some way to get Ruby to help you." She winked. "Maybe we can just trick the old bat. Anyway, now is not the time to discuss all this." She smiled sweetly. "I'm glad you're here. Why don't you clean up this place for me? I was looking forward to a summer of contentment and fun, and here you show up looking like a hunk of Swiss cheese." She slapped her thigh. "I knew I should have gone to see my nephew at Lake Ojibway. Here's the broom." She patted me on the shoulder and giggled. "I'm really glad to see you. You make me laugh. You really need those shields, but this will have to do for now." She suddenly threw a handful of cornmeal all over me. She'd had it concealed in her fist all this time. Then she tweaked my earring and said, "The earring will protect you from the neck up." And then she muttered, "I hope I never have to take on another white apprentice."

Agnes left to chop firewood. I swept the small cabin almost in a trance. It took a tremendous effort simply to move the table and chairs. Yet I felt compelled to do such a thorough job that I looked with extra care for every trace of dirt in the dark corners. There was plenty, and my brain felt just as dusty. I resented my docile compliance and felt more and more self-contempt. Agnes was taking an inordinately long time. I was so weary. The wind had come up and was droning through the high pine trees. Usually, the high sound of the wind was a thrilling event for me. Now it just intensified my feelings of loneliness. The cabin creaked and the shutter over the kitchen window started to bang. I went out and secured it shut. The smell of rain was in the air. A few hours ago I would have felt magic all around me. Now I felt only disenchantment. I looked up at the half moon and she seemed dimmed and distant. I was cold. Agnes's cabin looked shabby. Why was I here? I stumbled inside.

Agnes was preparing the night fire, gently poking and prodding it into life. I crawled wearily into my sleeping bag and fell into a deep sleep.

"It is dawn. Ah, you are no longer enchanted, my little wolf," Agnes said, standing over me. Was it morning already? I looked up at her. She looked like a most unmerciful angel. I just lay there with dull eyes, protecting my feelings by staring into space.

"Why, do I look disenchanted?" I asked weakly, not wanting her to know the extent of my vulnerability.

"Let's say that you appear on the inner lodges as listless, without energy and passion. It's as if there is an opening in the world within you. Your will has created that dark hole and your will must close it. *Your* will." Agnes grabbed the end of my sleeping bag and shook it so hard that I nearly tumbled out onto the floor. I scrambled to my feet and dressed hurriedly. The morning had come much too suddenly. I was ill-prepared to meet the day.

"Here." Agnes placed tea on the table. We ate breakfast in silence. Gray light was coming in through the window. The wind was still blowing. I was thinking about what Agnes had said, but somehow I didn't care. My mind was drifting. Maybe she was right. I had created a hole and felt caught in it. I had created my weakness and my apathy. The whole universe seemed like a major Broadway flop.

Agnes started to laugh. "It's your courage again. When I was your age, it happened to me. Not for the same reasons, but I lost my will. My being became soft. Don't worry, when you've chosen this road, it happens. It's a good sign."

I looked up at Agnes. She seemed old and unfamiliar.

"Why is it good? I feel dead."

"It's good because you are dying."

"Oh, that's wonderful, Agnes." I shook my head in disgust.

"You have chosen power, Lynn. Power has chosen you. Did I ever say that the medicine way was easy? Death is near you. You two are becoming acquainted. Know each other well. Death is all you have."

Each word she spoke threw me into a deeper depression. I got up and walked jerkily around the table, not wanting to think anymore.

"Come on, Lynn, we're driving over to Ruby's place. Bring my broom."

I picked up the old broom, thankful for the task, and followed Agnes to the car. I kept watching the ground and the damp earth as it collected on the toes of my boots. We drove in silence all the way to Ruby's cabin. I was relieved that no one was there.

"Lynn, clean the cabin while I go find Ruby." I went in and obediently started to sweep, concentrating on the sound of the

broom on the wooden plank floor. I swept, dusted, and washed a
heap of dirty dishes. Still, no one came back. Hours passed, or so it
seemed. I felt imprisoned. I collapsed on one of the bunks below an
open window and decided to take a nap. As I lay there, drifting off,
I thought I heard Ruby's rocking chair creaking outside on the
porch. Then I heard Agnes and Ruby cackling softly to each other.

"Well, Agnes, you sure have a live one this time. I can't believe
how gullible your apprentice is."

"You're right, Ruby, she sure is dumb."

I was struck by their derision. They were ridiculing me. I lay
there listening to them discuss my stupidity. They whispered
something to each other. What were they saying? All of a sudden
they burst into laughter. "And the way she wears her hair all
curled—we'll never make an Indian out of her." Agnes laughed
again.

"Well, at least you got a book out of her. I can't believe she came
back for more. Maybe I can get her to move old Jack's manure
pile." They laughed hysterically.

I'd had enough. I sprang up with a rage I didn't know I was
capable of and walked seething out on the porch. Agnes saw my
shadow and looked around. Her mock surprise infuriated me even
more.

"Oh, it's only you," she said.

"Yes, Agnes. It's only me. I'll be leaving now. I'm not going to
stick around where I'm not wanted."

I really was trying to hurt them both. I had been such a total
fool, swallowing everything with wide, starry eyes. What an
imbecile! They were right. I was stupid. If this was a path of
knowledge, I didn't want any part of it. I whirled around and headed
for the car.

"Oh, let me walk you to your car, Lynn." Agnes leapt up and
followed directly on my heels. I began to run and she kept right in
step with me, nearly driving me mad.

"Stop running on top of me," I yelled, and turned around sharply
to glare at Agnes. She was standing about ten feet from me. I was
stunned because I was sure she was on my tail. I turned away from

her with a snort of disgust, when suddenly my feet became tangled together as if they had been hobbled. In an instant I was face down in the dirt. The wind was knocked out of me. A hot, pulsing stickiness crawled over my skin. Agnes said, "I think I'll let you go back and gather your stuff alone. I sure hope you drive better than you walk." She turned on her heel and walked jauntily back to Ruby's cabin.

As I sat up in the dirt, spitting out sand and brushing myself off, I suddenly realized that I couldn't leave. In my fit of anger, I had forgotten about Red Dog and what Storm had told me at the Beverly Hills Hotel. More tears of anger and frustration stung my eyelids. Like a beaten pup looking for food, I slowly padded back to Ruby's cabin and walked in on them both sitting at the table looking at me expectantly, as if they knew I'd return. I sat down and blurted out the whole experience at the hotel. When I was finished, there was a long silence. Then Agnes and Ruby both came over to me and put their arms around me, laughing, trying to tickle me, and wiping away my tears.

"Boy, do you need drama!" laughed Ruby. "We needed to wake you up."

"I don't understand," I said, bewildered by their change in attitude.

"We wondered when you'd get around to telling us," Agnes said with mock indignation.

"I tried to tell you. Do you mean that you knew?"

"Who did you think that was talking in your head, the cleaning lady?" Agnes laughed at my expression.

"So that really was you. How could Red Dog show up in a limousine dressed like that? He looked magnificent."

"That's a favorite trick of sorcerers, to turn up where you least expect to find them. He chose that particular form as a way of throwing you out of your fixed notions. Sorcerers can move in any direction, and sometimes in many directions at once." Agnes smiled and shook her head. "It was easy for him to look like a gentleman—he was once known as Father Pierson, a priest."

"Yes, of course." I remembered the license plate on his limousine that read, "FATHER." Red Dog must have thought that quite a good joke.

Agnes smiled. "He knows how to behave in so-called civilized society. He knows the pictures people carry in their heads of the way things and people ought to look. He can look comfortable almost anywhere. It's really simple."

I was starting to feel a twinge of pricked ego again, and I resolved to be much more careful in the future.

"Agnes, the whole scary event pointed out for me how much further I have to go. I just couldn't handle it. I forgot all my training. I couldn't apply any of it. You didn't tell me all his powers." I caught myself wanting to blame Agnes again. "Agnes, I started to blame you because I'm frightened." I perched on my chair, holding my knees to my chest, and rocked back and forth. Agnes made a clicking noise with her tongue and squinted one eye. She wasn't reacting to my fear, which made me feel even more foolish. Ruby lay down on her bed to sleep. We picked up our things, said goodbye, and left. We continued talking all the way back to the cabin.

"I always told you, Lynn, once you take power, you have to keep it. The having is one thing. The holding is another." She paused and held her left hand up palm open, and then placed her right hand over it, palm down. Then she held both up in a triumphant gesture. "The feminine part of each of us, male or female, needs to be allowed to operate. Learn to receive, learn to hold. Now I'm not saying clutch. I'm saying *hold*. A big difference."

"But how could the spiritual part of the basket be taken from me? It's part of me now."

"By killing you." Agnes saw the terror in my eyes. "If he can. But he must do that in what he thinks is an honorable way. He must deceive you. Oh, he won't just blow you up or shoot you. That would be too easy. You have stolen his woman power and he wants her back. He won't take what you've done lying down. He'll do almost anything. What was difficult for you will be easy for him. Remember, he's a great sorcerer and totally dedicated to his art. When you first arrived here, you were half dead. Now that you're

stirred up and frightened and angry, you're alive again." She
chuckled. "For a while anyway." She got up and stood over me,
looking over my body carefully. "You've got more holes in you than
a treaty." A new look of seriousness replaced her smile. "I can see
that you've left the path, Lynn. That is why we were so hard on
you. We had to bring you back. You think you've accomplished
something with your book. You're self-satisfied. And that's when you
enter into real danger."

I heard my voice. It sounded small and whiney, like a child's
voice. "But I've done just what you've told me to do. Wasn't that an
act of power?"

"Yes. And in writing the story of your experience, you have given
some women a tool for going beyond. Women need that. If a
woman makes an act of power, she's created someting like a work of
art. It changes her forever. It gives her new vision on this mother
earth, teaches her to see. Teaches her to know what she feels and
teaches her to feel what she knows. When that happens, she can
recreate herself. She knows what she wants, what is necessary, and
she knows what she doesn't want, what's unnecessary. In the process
of sharing your story with others, you have been lured off the path.
You have forgotten where you stand on the medicine wheel. You
are off the path." I parked the car by the cabin and we got out.

"But, Agnes." I floundered for the right words as I followed her
down the trail. "Agnes, your teachings are all that I've thought of."

"My teachings are not important if you have left the path."

"But I don't know what I've done. I'm still dedicated to
knowledge."

"Yes, but knowledge is not enough," Agnes said as we went into
the cabin. She sat down and faced me. "You don't yet fully
understand your knowledge, and understanding can't be taught. It
just comes. And so knowledge sits in your head like uncooked food
on a stove." Agnes got up and walked to the stove, lit it, and stirred
some soup with a wooden spoon as she spoke. "You think you're on
the right trail, but you're not. You're lost. You think you know a lot
now. But you know less and less."

"What can I do?"

"Well, you're going to have to do whatever I tell you." She
stopped stirring the soup. "Maybe I'll read you."

"What do you mean?"

"We're going to have a crystal ceremony, so I can see into you
and see what's gone wrong."

"I didn't know you still worked with crystals."

"There's a lot you don't know."

She portioned out the soup into two wooden bowls as soon as it
was hot. "Here. Eat. Let my stirring of the soup stir you into that
quiet place." I watched her hand as it stirred, and it did in fact seem
to quiet my taut nerves. We ate in silence and then went outside.

The shadows lengthened over the clearing around the cabin as I
sat with Agnes on the porch. I watched her expression change in the
waning light, the lines on her face deepening and then almost
disappearing. Her eyes were closed, resting. I felt more peaceful,
grateful that fate had allowed me to know this strange woman.

"Movement," Agnes uttered the word, elongating the sounds of
the letters. She didn't open her eyes nor did she move. "Movement,
movement, movement," she kept repeating the word in a monotone.

"Movement?" I asked.

"Movement, movement," she pulled out the vowel sounds in a
sort of humming.

"Do you want me to move, Agnes?"

"I want you to listen to the sound behind my words. Sound holds
the world together. Movement, movement," she kept repeating.

I tried to listen carefully. Her tone had an odd, gutteral quality
that pulled at my memory.

"Movement, movement." Slowly Agnes opened her eyes to watch
me and she started to giggle.

"Why are you laughing?"

"All the blood is rushing to your head!"

I laughed, realizing that I was straining my facial muscles trying
to understand what she wanted.

"Look, listen from here." Agnes patted her solar plexus.

"Movement." She repeated herself fifty or sixty times. "I am
holding a thought behind my word. See if you can reach it with

your dream body." She patted her belly again, repeating the word hypnotically.

"I can't see anything," I said, deflated.

"You have to drop your mind for this and hear only with your body. Clear your mind. Try again. You'll see. Again she repeated, "Movement, movement, movement."

This time I saw or sensed a medicine wheel in the sound and made out a circle of stones. I felt myself moving from trust and innocence in the south of the wheel to wisdom and strength in the north. I saw a moose standing at the top of the wheel as I moved upwards. Agnes stopped speaking and watched me, a comical look on her face. I opened my eyes and shut them, blinking frantically because the image had stayed with me. Slowly, it faded.

"See? Simple." Agnes dusted her palms together and we laughed. It was almost completely dark when we went into the cabin. We stopped by the fire and sat down at the table, lighting a lamp.

"That was like a hallucination."

"It's just another way of looking. It is better to look with your dream body when something is important, because your eyes can be tricked and your own mind can fool you. You don't have to tell me what you saw—a medicine wheel of stones, and you moved toward the north, right?"

"Agnes, yes, and much more." Now I was excited. "I understood what you've told me about movement. I never really understood what you said about the need for movement to occur before you can transform yourself from substance into spirit. Now I see, but I can't really explain how I see it."

"That's the point. There are some things you can't explain with words. That's why you must learn two ways of looking—one with your eyes and one with your dream body." Agnes reached over and rubbed my stomach. I realized it was a little bit tender.

"Agnes, you make things very difficult for me."

Agnes turned her head sideways, like a magpie, and stared. "I do?"

"What just happened—I want to share that experience with people through my writing. But how can I really explain it?"

"I never said it would be easy." Agnes got up and started making herb tea.

"Book reviewers and anthropologists—even some Indians—don't understand what I write about you and Ruby."

"Why is that?" Agnes was smiling and drumming her fingers on the counter.

"Because they think your behavior is too changeable: one minute you're brilliant philosophers and the next you act like bickering housewives from Winnepeg. One minute you are medicine women, making me walk through the valley of death, and the next minute you roll around like children. I guess it's hard for people to understand."

There was a long silence as Agnes set the tea on the table. She heaved a big sigh as she sat down. "The world sees the Indians as a conquered people. The world sees us as small men and women confined to the tribal borders, victims on the reservation. It was not long ago that we were murdered for performing the Ghost Dance. Our real power is hidden. It had to be if we were to preserve it. Not only has the person of power had the white world to fear, but Indians turned against Indians out of fear. You know all this, but sometimes you forget. Often our own people don't recognize us. We stay hidden. We have to. But we travel and meet with each other. We share knowledge, and it has always been that way. If an apprentice needs to learn about kachinas, for instance, we may send them on the good red road to the south to the pueblos. Why do your educators think that's so odd?"

"They seem to think that if you're a Cree, that's all you relate to."

"If you have a student who wants to learn about France, don't you send her to France?"

"Yes."

"Well, it's the same for some of us. Of course, there are some medicine people who stay just with their nation. That is their way and I honor them. Medicine people all have their own ideas and they must be respected.

"You are full of words and borrowed knowledge from the white system. That has its purpose. But here we make you *live* what we want you to learn. That's why we change personalities. Because we *are* the teaching. We don't stand up at a podium and lecture you about truth. We make you feel and breathe truth, become it. You have to react to our play and that starts you down a road."

"But that's so hard to explain to people."

"Every book is rewritten by the reader. If you read a book, it becomes your personal teacher. You bring to it what you are."

"I guess they'll find what they need."

"That's right. Now let's get some sleep. We have a long day tomorrow."

Moments later in my sleeping bag, I could hear Agnes's even breathing. She was already asleep. The trees outside brushed back and forth over the old boards of the cabin like pebbles caught in the tide. I listened until the harmony on the far side of the wind lulled me to sleep.

I woke to see Agnes open the door of her cabin and take a deep breath. I felt her lungs expand in joy, as if I were part of her body. The sun bathed her in a soft, tender light. She looked radiant. When she finally spoke, her voice had a musical tone. Something in it made me feel gladness throughout my body. I got up, and we prepared what she called "meagers"—a breakfast of tea and porridge.

"Lynn, when you realize that life is magical, then and only then can you begin to practice magic." Her voice seemed to come from each corner of the room. "Women need a form that is a counterpart of the male form, but one that is truly their own. In emulating men, women give up their power, their specialness.

"But there is more. I can't heal you if I am disconnected from you. I need to touch your spirit, see into you. I will use the crystal helpers to do this. Crystals teach you essence and true beginnings. When you know the beginnings, crystals will teach you to see more and more. Within the crystal is a flame—you can be drawn into that fire, a fire that cleanses the heart of motives and makes you open. At that point, I will truly see you."

Agnes went to the window and closed it. She motioned for me to get my bedroll. "Gather what you think you may need for a couple of days, Lynn." I was still tired from my journey to Manitoba, but I knew better than to protest.

We were soon driving south, bouncing down the bumpy road in my rented car. Twilight was lingering over the lonely plains of Manitoba. Low trees formed strange configurations in the golden light. Abruptly, Agnes directed me to turn west on a rutted dirt road. From that turn we drove for miles in silence. Just as the sun gave the last bit of itself to the day, we made a turn towards a strange outcropping of rocks that were jumbled together like arthritic knuckles.

Just below the rocks was a fenced-in pasture. Agnes told me to pull over beside it, a few feet off the road. I looked around. There was no evidence of anyone in any direction. We gathered our things, and held the barbed wire open for each other. I had no idea of where we were heading. In the dim light, I could see the outline of a buffalo standing near the rocks. I quickly walked closer to Agnes. She laughed, knowing my trepidation.

"Where are we going?" I asked. My attention was caught by a flicker of grey smoke. When I looked up, I saw smoke spiraling from the top of a hill.

"We're going to my cousin's lodge."

It was nearly dark as we walked around the low hill to the east. Suddenly, I realized that the "hill" was actually a huge earth lodge. We walked until we came to an opening in the mound that had an old buffalo hide hanging over it. It reminded me of an opening into a mine shaft.

"Wait here," Agnes ordered, and then she disappeared into the mound. Moments later she called me to enter. I pushed the buffalo hide back and stepped into a ribbed tunnel that led me down about four or five feet into the earth. I entered a round dwelling about forty feet across. A fire pit dug out of the center was filled with burning coals. The smoke went up through a hole in the center of the dome fourteen feet or so above us. Agnes began tending the fire.

"This is Grandmother Walking Stick's lodge, my Choctaw cousin. She is a crystal medicine woman, a stone woman. She's not here, but we are welcome. Put your bedroll over there." Agnes indicated a sort of rack extending on legs from a shelf that ran the circumference of the lodge.

I was awed by what I saw; four big poles held up the roof. Elaborately painted buffalo hides hung from two rafters. I saw all kinds of wonderful objects—more painted buffalo skins, Indian rugs, and many animal skins spread over the dirt floors. The lodge had a great and simple beauty. I looked up at the smoke hole, which only moments before I had taken for a camp fire on a hill. I wondered how many other things I failed to see because I saw them with my customary preconceptions.

As I looked around, I saw that the lodge was much like a Pawnee structure. "What is this kind of lodge doing in Canada?" I asked Agnes.

"My cousin came from Oklahoma, long ago, and has always preferred to live this way. Come sit and let us talk awhile." She patted the rug next to her.

I settled near her, our feet warmed by the fire.

"Closer."

I moved closer. Agnes peered into the fire.

"You're wondering why I brought you all the way out here."

"Yes."

"We are all here to learn, but you are here to learn much that is specific. Often what we are supposed to learn is not clear at first."

I watched her beautiful old face as the firelight danced on it, casting a large black shadow on the painted buffalo hide behind her. I wanted to cry out for the sheer beauty of Agnes and her people. I felt as though I had gone centuries back in time. Tears of gratitude rolled down my cheeks. She covered my hand with hers.

We drank some Navajo tea that I had brought her and ate bologna sandwiches. We laughed and talked for several hours about all the things that had happened in the past. She assured me that she and Ruby had not meant the awful things they had said. "We had to make you really hurt and angry to wake up your power," she said. She unrolled a blanket containing many pouches filled with crystals of varying sizes. One by one she laid them out between us and told me where each was from, and which ones were male, female, or neutral. They represented many of the sacred mountains of the world. Soon we went outside and put several crystals on a tripod that was standing near the lodge.

"Grandmother Moon will awaken them tonight. When women work with crystals, it is Grandmother Moon you speak to. Grandfather Sun awakens crystals used by men."

We went back inside the lodge. Agnes handed me four crystals.

"Here," she said. "Sleep with these. It is good to trade your energy."

I crawled into my sleeping bag, putting one crystal at my head, one at my feet, and holding the others. I shut my eyes and was soon sound asleep. I dreamed about pyramids with the full moon over the pinnacle.

I had rested well, the crystals still in my hands. I was relaxed, and my level of energy had certainly risen. Waking up in an earth lodge is like being reborn. The earth is a wonderful insulation against heat, cold, and sound.

Light momentarily flooded the lodge as Agnes walked up the tunnel and outside. I got up quickly and rolled up my sleeping bag, placing the crystals on a blanket. I made tea, and sat on the otter skin rug to drink it. Stillness pervaded everything.

Agnes soon returned, informing me that it was early in the afternoon and that I had needed my rest.

"What does Grandmother Walking Stick do with these hides?" I asked. "I believe her work could be quite valuable. Do you suppose she would want to exhibit them?"

"Never," Agnes said with humor. She made a gesture indicating that I should examine the hides more closely. "Much of the way of the people has been told in legend. Much has been woven into the medicine belts. Much has been forgotten. But there are some who have the ability to remember. Grandmother Walking Stick is a memorizer who remembers the trail for her people. She paints stories onto the buffalo hide. To my knowledge, no other white person has ever seen these. She knew you would be coming and could have rolled them out of sight. The crystals told her to trust you. It is a great honor. Grandmother Walking Stick is a great warrioress and teacher, and you may have the honor of meeting her one day."

On one of the hide paintings there was a strange figure of a woman with a cluster of people sitting around her. The woman had a rather flat forehead, like a Mayan, and a twist of hair that juted forward in a curious hornlike fashion.

"Agnes, what does this figure represent?"

"She is a twisted hair. In the days before the white man came, twisted hairs—wandering storytellers—went all over this turtle island. Everyone loved them—their special medicine. I think you would have been a twisted hair in those old times. Instead of writing a book, you would have gone from village to village. The twisted hairs were loved wherever they went because of their great talent. At night around the fires the whole village would come to be entertained and to learn. They knew many stories and collected them.

"It is hard now to imagine the power of the twisted hair. She could convincingly take on the voice of anyone. She could make you think you were talking to the wind or plants or animals. Whether she signed or spoke, a twisted hair could take you into her special world and make you forget everything. Twisted hairs were the chief conjurers. Would you like to hear a story that I heard once? It was told by one of the last twisted hairs, Yellow Robe."

"Yes, very much."

"I will tell you the story Yellow Robe told. Get comfortable."

I lay down on my back watching the clouds through the smokehole.

"Imagine you are very tired. The whole village is waiting for Yellow Robe, waiting very respectfully. Pretty soon she comes out and she tells some funny stories. Then she begins to talk about herself. 'My name is Yellow Robe. I was born in the north and then I grew up among the People of the Lakes. When I was twelve years old I went to live with my aunt in the western camps. Her name was Day Owl. Because of her vision, Aunt Day Owl had pledged that she would walk the Great Salt Road to the Mayan cities of the far south and learn medicine from them. I begged her to let me accompany her and she consented.

" 'We canoed most of the way. We went down the Grandfather
River. We caught a ride on an ocean-going canoe and we traveled
for fifteen days. From that point on we walked. We joined a caravan
of traders. Everyone knew that we were on a sacred mission, for we
carried the Mayan Talk Shield. On the face of the shield were
painted four jaguars and four eagles.

" 'When we began the journey, my aunt was quite a large
woman. But as we traveled she became skinny—it surprises me yet
how beautiful Aunt Day Owl became! She had also been a woman
who was not very healthy, but she became very strong during the
trip.

" 'We traveled to five villages, staying at each village for one year.
I was just going on my seventeenth summer when we were invited
by a powerful medicine woman named Pipe to go to the City of the
Corn Dancers. Aunt Day Owl and I went there and we stayed. I
joined the Society of Learning of the Medicine Bow. All my
learning was within the Society.

" 'When I was twenty-two summers old, I went to my aunt. I had
a problem. "Auntie," I told her. "There is a certain young man that
I am having a very hard time talking to."

" ' "Who is he?" Aunt Day Owl asked.

" ' "His name is Golden Sand, but I just call him Sand."

" 'Aunt Day Owl smiled. "Golden Sand is the son of Thunder
Child. Why can't you speak with him? Is it because he is so very
handsome?"

" 'I must have blushed deeply. "No—it is because of Arrow Light,
his brother. He does not like me and he wants to keep us apart. I
don't care if I talk to Sand or not."

" ' "I will do what I can," Aunt Day Owl said.

" 'A long time passed and I didn't hear anything. I was pining
away. I think I even lost weight. Golden Sand was strong as a
jaguar. His eyes were so kind and pure in spirit that they truly
possessed me. The graceful way he moved caused a melody of
energy to pass from one person to the next.

" 'Arrow Light, his brother, was one year older than me. He
belonged to the Bow Society, too. I thought that he didn't like me,

because he was very severe with me while he taught me. He would make me work long hours. He would never tolerate it if I slowed down even for a moment.

" 'One day I had to place fifty arrows through the Ball Court hoop and not touch the sides, shooting from one hundred meters. The reason Arrow Light ordered me to do that was because I had missed one rolling hoop that day.

" 'I used to think about Sand constantly. He seemed to be in my heart from the time I woke up until I went to bed. It was driving me crazy. When I could stand it no longer, I walked up to Arrow Light and told him I loved his brother and that if he didn't like it he could meet me on the Ball Court to see who would be whose slave!

" 'Arrow Light laughed so hard that he had to sit down. I was so angry that I struck the ground and shattered the bow that was in my hands.

" 'You are a foolish girl,' Arrow Light said. "My family had already talked to your aunt and they had given away seven Quetzal Robes for the challenge day.

" ' "What challenge day?" I asked.

" ' "Silence," he ordered. "You know the rule of silence."

" 'The rule was that I could not question my Bow Chief about any matter other than the meditation of the bow.

" 'Agonizing months went by. Then one day a chief came to the Ball courts and called the Society together. He said, "Members, bowmen, and bowwomen, the challenge day has arrived. It is the custom to give away the greatest prize the people have collectively. This year our give away is the warrior Golden Sand and the warrioress Rain. They have agreed to marry the female and male Mask winners respectively."

" 'Not one of us were Mayan. No one knew exactly what the chief was talking about. So we had to wait, but not long. Four days later, we were again called to the Ball Court. The Master Bowwoman addressed us.

" ' "Bowmen and bowwomen," she said. "Tomorrow begins the games. You will compete in this Ball Court for your place in the Great Race."

" 'No one had the slightest idea what he meant by the "Great

Race," but we were warriors and as such we were eager to compete.

" 'We assembled the following day at the Ball Court. Hundreds and hundreds of people were there. We did not expect to see the crowd. Golden Sand and Rain were brought in Quetzal Chairs and sat down at the place of honor at the place of the jaguar. That is the place of the balance of forgetting and remembering—very sacred to the Mayan.

" 'The games began. We were pitted against one another, but there were no losers. Our starting position in the race was won according to how well we did in competition. Seeing Golden Sand made me extremely agitated, and I unsuccessfully tried to use my willpower not to think about him.

" 'Fifty-three men and women competed for the race. I was the last. In other words, wherever we were going to race to, I had to start out last. Nobody knew where we were going to race to or for what reason.

" 'That night, another chief came to our camp. "Bowmen and bowwomen," he said, "the race will begin tomorrow. Here are the rules. Each of you will be given a stick. On the stick is a mark."

" 'The chief stopped talking and sat down. Five men and five women began to hand out small carved sticks. Each stick had a carved jaguar head on it. There were fifty-three marks on my stick; I counted them. After the sticks were passed out, the chief stood up again.

" ' "Only one bowwoman has broken the rule," he began. "Her name is Yellow Robe. She spoke to her Bow Chief, asking him a personal question. Because of that, Yellow Robe will be made to wait longer by one hundred counts.

" ' "Each man and woman will stand in a line with his brothers and sisters, shoulder to shoulder. The Counting Chiefs will call out each of your names according to the counting sticks. A name will be called, and the Counting Chief will count to one hundred. After you hear your name and the count ends, you must place seven arrows through the Ball Court hoop at fifty paces.

" ' "Then you will run to the Sun River. There you will place six arrows through the moving hoop of the Owl Chiefs. From there you will follow the jaguar flags. Those flags will take you all the way to your goal. The next stop is at the Stone Chief. Place five arrows through the swinging hoop.

" ' "Next you will run up the Flower Mountain. There you will find the Eagle Chiefs. Place four arrows through their moving hoop. From there you will run to the Blue Meadow. Place three arrows through the moving hoop of the White Shell Chiefs. There is a long valley beyond the Blue Meadow. Run to that Valley to Sun Gate. Place two arrows through that moving hoop. You must then find your mask, the one that has your mark upon it. After you have picked up your mask, run back to the Ball Court. Throw the mask at the feet of the Quetzalcoatl. Then place one arrow through the Ball Court hoop.

" ' "Anyone not making it back to the Ball Court will be flogged and made to be a ten-year slave. Judges will then consider your race. Their decision is final. No questions will be asked, for that is the law.

" ' "If there is any bowman or bowwoman here who does not want to run the race, speak now. Your stick will be removed. If you wait until tomorrow to decide, you will receive five lashes with the whip, then be released to return to your home.

" ' "Nothing will be repeated. It is the law. You have been trained to remember. You are great bowmen and bowwomen. It is the wish of all the chiefs that you find your understanding in this final race. I have spoken."

" 'Only one man immediately spoke up and excused himself. The following morning, six others excused themselves. They were flogged and told to return home. I spoke with each of those men and women later—all of them had become nervous and forgotten the instructions.

" 'I was now number forty-six, a slight improvement. The game began. One by one, as the names were called, players ran forward. I watched. Everyone watched. The first man was slow and he kept missing. The second person was a woman, who seemed to be even worse. There were three now trying to place their arrows through the hoop all at once. Suddenly, a horn blew.

" ' "Stop the games!" a chief yelled. "Dishonor!" He pointed to two of the men who had been trying to get their arrows through. The two men he had pointed at had started to run. They had cheated. They had assumed that the many arrows would be confused, but they were not. These two were eliminated.

" 'The horn blew again. Three more were eliminated. I began to wonder how the heralders could keep so accurate a count. Each of our arrows was painted differently, and had different colored feathers. The eye of the bowman is trained for many years to discern movement, color, size, and where any object will ultimately go. We did not know that those heralders to the Game Chiefs were also bowmen and bowwomen undergoing their own test.

" 'When I finally had my turn, there were eleven still shooting. I took my time, but many of my arrows were deflected. I had to use sixteen arrows to finally get seven through. I ran as fast as I could go to the next test—the Hoop of the Owls. When I got there, I was so out of breath I could not pull my bow. I had to sit down and get back my strength. That time I shot fifteen arrows before I could get six through.

" 'I ran, trotted, and walked to the next hoop—the Hoop of the Stone Chiefs. I had to use eight arrows to get five through. We were given more arrows at each place where we were tested. The next stop was the Eagle Chiefs. I did as before, conserving my strength. I even stopped once to drink a little water. I saw a man, a brother, limping along. He had gotten cactus needles in his foot. I made him sit down and I helped him pull them out. Others passed by us as I did so.

" 'Before long, I removed all the needles and we both took off running again. The injured man was fast and soon was far ahead of me. I took my time. It was much further to the Eagle Chiefs than I had anticipated. I passed many bowmen and bowwomen as I walked. When I got to the Hoop of the Eagle Chiefs, I was careful. I took only four pulls and put four arrows through.

" 'It was even further to the Hoop of the White Shell Chiefs. The sun was high before I got there. I was tired and thirsty. I had not realized how tired I was, and I fell asleep. The world around me

became a world of color and sound. I didn't know where I was.
Light was streaming from a glowing circle in front of me. When I
faced the light, I saw it was a warrioress carrying a gold shield and
spear.

" ' "Who are you?" I asked.

" ' "I am she who nourishes," she answered.

" 'She was beautiful and her perfume filled the air—it was a most
fragrant smell. Her face was so radiant, I was in awe.

" ' "Are you a goddess or are you a human, like me?"

" ' "I am she who walks with you to show you the road," she said.
"Through me, you can be initiated. Through me, you can taste
victory."

" ' "Walk last and pick up the burdens of the people. No woman
is worthy until she follows her heart."

" 'As soon as she said this, her shield began to glow like the sun
and I became frightened. I awoke with a start and realized that the
sun, which had been beating down on me, had lowered
considerably. I drank some water, enough to quench my thirst, and
began to walk. I never passed one man or woman, and it began to
worry me. I reached the place of the White Shell Chiefs in the late
afternoon. I shot my three arrows through the hoop and sat down
and rested. I had one more moving hoop to go—the Sun Gate. It
was downhill and I was trotting and walking, but even then I had to
sit down every once in a while and rest. I never passed one person.

" 'It was dark by the time I reached the Sun Gate, but the hoop
was lit with torches. I saw nine bowmen and bowwomen asleep
there. I placed my two arrows through the hoop and I started back.
Suddenly, I remembered the masks. There were five masks left. It
took a little time to count and make sure that I had the right mask.
A chief held up a torch so that I could see.

" 'I nearly fell on my head when I picked up the mask. It was
very, very heavy. My mask was made out of solid gold. That is
heavy, believe me. It took me nearly an hour to strip the bark I
needed to make a sling. I hung the mask on my back and started
back for the Ball Courts.

" 'The further I walked, the heavier the gold mask seemed to become. I passed two women who were carrying their masks in their arms. I shouted to them to make slings.

" 'I was very upset. It was all I could do to put one tired foot in front of the other. I found it almost impossible to breathe. The going was very slow. By now it was very dark. If the flags had not been there, I would have easily become lost.

" 'I was weak, and I tripped and stumbled many times. It seemed like the path was extremely steep, and at times I thought I was going to have to crawl. I wondered if the flags were leading to some other destination rather than the Ball Courts.

" 'Dawn was just beginning to streak the horizon when an old woman stopped me. "Please, my daughter," she pleaded. "I am sick, can you not help me?"

" 'Fumbling, I stopped and gave her water. She was grateful.

" ' "You should be back in your camp," I said. "Why are you out here alone?"

" ' "I have been here all night," she answered. "I live alone with my tiny granddaughter. I was out gathering wood when I twisted my ankle. I'm afraid my granddaughter may be in danger of hurting herself."

" 'She looked at me imploringly. I stood there, torn between helping her and sending help back for her. I explained that I was in the great competition. She then insisted that I go and send back help. I could see she was suffering. I went into the nearby trees and I began to make a travois to pull her back to her camp.

" 'The sun was high above the horizon before I had completed my work. I knew I had lost the race, and so I did not bother to hurry—yet, pressed on. Clumsily, I pulled her to the camp and helped her into her lodge. She thanked me and went inside. I was only about five steps away when she called to me. "Eat this as you walk," she said. "Keep courage, my daughter. Nothing can change the outcome of the race." She handed me a bright red scarf that was filled with fruit. I took it with trembling fingers and thanked her for her kindness.

" 'I realized I was no longer able to think clearly. I walked to the Ball Court eating the fruit. I was half starved. There were only twenty or thirty people there when I arrived. I placed my mask and shot my last arrow through the hoop. Then I went to my lodge and went to sleep. No one had spoken a word when I completed the race. I wanted to ask many questions, but, as it was forbidden, I did not.

" 'I slept until nightfall. I woke up feeling impatient. I was annoyed when I thought back over the race. I walked around for awhile, and then had a bite to eat. I became tired again and I went back to sleep.

" 'The following morning I was shaken awake and told to go to the Ball Courts. I got dressed and left. I took my place at the Line of Contention; this was at the Place of the Eagle. I counted the bowmen and bowwomen who stood with me; there were thirty, fifteen men and fifteen women.

" 'About one hundred chiefs with bright plumed headdresses and gold ornaments were seated along one side of the Court. The garments they wore were red. We stood in silence—waiting. After what seemed an endless amount of time, fifty-three old women came into the area known as the Fire Keeper. It is said to be the Place of Purity. A large bowl of water and a large bowl of fire marked that place.

" 'I had seen those women before; they came many times to watch us practice with our bows. Each time they came, the old women wore masks of Earth, Air, Fire, and Water. I was quite used to seeing them.

" 'Still we waited, and others came and sat in chosen places of honor. Then the horn blew. Twenty chiefs came into the Court—they were all dressed in the Quetzal Robes.

" 'One of the chiefs stepped forward. "The race has ended," he announced. "Now each of the remaining bowmen and bowwomen will come forward and ask one personal question. They will whisper that question to the Quetzal Chiefs so only we will hear." He sat back down.

We knew the rule: we would walk forward one by one, beginning at the left and going down the ranks to the right. I was somewhere in the middle. The closer my time came to speak, the more frustrated I became. I loved Golden Sand more than I could ever express. I knew that I was defeated, but my heart would not let him go.

" 'When my time came, I walked up to the Quetzal Chiefs. My words spilled out of me. "Now that I have lost," I whispered, "Is there anything I can do to marry Golden Sand? I love him."

" 'Of course, the Quetzal Chiefs never answered—just as they did not answer the others. I walked back and took my place in the Line of Contention. The Quetzal Chiefs filed out, and so did the old women. A Bow Chief told us to sit down on the ground. We did.

" 'Soon we were fed and given sweet drink—the cocoa. It was noon before the Quetzal Chiefs returned. Behind them, the Hoop Chiefs filed in. The Sun Gate Chiefs, the White Shell Chiefs, the Eagle Chiefs, the Stone Chiefs, and the Owl Chiefs—in that order, they all sat down. The old women came next, but they had removed their masks. I recognized one of them as the old woman I had helped. She was not limping.

" 'The chief of the old women stood up, and she began to call out our names. I was last. After she had called out our names, she sat back down. One of the Quetzal Chiefs rose to his feet. "You will all receive an extra gift," he announced to us. "As we call your name, come up and receive your gift."

" 'An Owl Chief stood up. He began to call out the names. As each man and woman went forward, the old women would place a beautiful shawl about their shoulders. Then each man and woman was handed a magnificent bow and quiver of arrows. The warrioress Rain was awarded to the last bowman.

" 'I was now the only bowwoman left standing.

" 'A Sun Gate Chief stood up.

" ' "Each of you," he said, "showed signs of kindness. You helped your brothers and sisters—for this we honor you. All of you have won the race. The woman Yellow Robe we honor the most. She not only was kind to her sisters and brothers, she was the only one that helped her Grandmother. For this help she has rendered to her Grandparent, she now becomes the wife of Golden Sand!" Everyone stood and cheered. I wept for joy.

" 'Golden Sand is now a medicine man. I depend on him for my very life. He works with the powers of the north. Golden Sand has stood right beside me through all these years. When we are not together, I speak in prayer to him. He has been my heart and my strength. He believed in me and cared for me. He made medicine for me.' "

I opened my eyes as Agnes finished the story. I had been dreaming along with her. We talked for a long time about the twisted hairs and the sacredness of their teaching stories. Agnes insisted that twisted hairs was one of my medicines, and she said that in the old days I would have walked the great salt road and told tales to all the people. She explained that Walking Stick was one of the last living twisted hairs, but that now she preferred painting her stories on buffalo hides to telling them orally. I realized that there were very few people, even Indians, who knew of Walking Stick. To the profane, her real function was disguised. If a curious anthropologist or reporter came poking around, they would be told that Walking Stick raised buffalo and nothing more.

Agnes and I went for a walk a short distance from Walking Stick's lodge. Agnes had ordered me to bring along two fruit jars and forbade me to ask any questions. We walked to the south of an outcropping of rocks and came to a flowing spring. The area around the spring was swampy and I became conscious of the buzzing insects.

"Get two jars of water," Agnes said.

By this time it was late afternoon. I carried the jars in front of me, trying not to splash the water out. Walking Stick had a full water can, so I wondered why we were filling the jars. I was famished, but Agnes told me not to eat. She said that I could drink the Navajo tea using the water from the water can. I was also told to keep the fruit jars containing the spring water near me at all times; until she asked for it, she said, keeping the jars happy was a warrioress's responsibility. Spring water is good because it is from a place of origin.

"Crystal Woman is here in spirit," Agnes said, taking a bundle from beside the firepit and unwrapping it. She lifted up a white dress made out of pieces of sewn deer hide. It had very simple stitching and was sunbleached to a pure white.

"You must wear only white," she said. "Here. Walking Stick made this for you herself. She knows things that will be. . . ."

"But how does she know?"

"Crystal Woman talks often to her. Put the dress on."

Agnes took out a pouch as I was changing clothes. She began to prepare the ground by waving a large feather over it.

"Take off all your jewelry. Wear nothing that is not white. Wrap them up and put them out of sight."

"Why do I do that, Agnes?"

"Because Crystal Woman hates shiny things. She will not come if anything will melt her power. Help me light these lamps."

I lit both lamps. Agnes was moving the fire container, a fifty-five-gallon oil drum cut off about a foot-and-a-half high and laying on the floor of the middle of the earth lodge. We carried it and all metal objects outside. Agnes worked methodically, rolling back the skins and woven rugs, placing them on the ledge and exposing the earth floor. She took out a large pouch and etched a circle with a stick directly below the smoke hole. She continually looked up at the hole as she did this. She poured a large amount of a yellow-white substance in the etched circle.

"What is that," I asked.

"That is corn pollen," she said.

When she was finished, she had a large, circular mound of pollen directly under the smoke hole.

"I want you to go outside with your jars of water and wait until I call you. While you are waiting I will prepare the Lizard Trail."

"What is the Lizard Trail?"

"I will explain everything you need to know when we are calling down Crystal Woman. It has to be done at a special moment. Crystal Woman is related to a certain distant star that I will point out to you sometime. Now leave the earth lodge. Do not drop or spill your jars of water. If you do, it's bad medicine. Listen while you wait to hear the voice of the sister wind. She often chants before the calling of Crystal Woman."

Agnes had dismissed me. I took the two jars of water, careful not
to spill them, and went outside. I sat down not far from the
entrance and leaned my back against a clump of buffalo grass. The
stars were out—it seemed like the whole Milky Way—and the moon
was low over the hills. The scent of flowers and grass filled the air. I
was aware of every small sound. The wind picked up and did indeed
seem to be chanting, emitting a soft, feminine, trilling whistle that
gave me a most pleasant sensation as the breath of wind caressed
me. I relaxed and let the chanting of the wind soothe me. Then the
sound became shrill and disappeared. The suddenness of it jarred
me to alertness.

"Lynn, the Lizard Trail is prepared. Bring your jars of water and
do everything exactly as I tell you."

Agnes held back the buffalo hide for me and I entered with my
jars. One dim candle was burning, and I was struck with the
sensation that inside of the lodge, reality was drastically different. I
stood just inside. In the center, sitting on the mound of corn pollen,
was a huge crystal. Directly in front of me was a star, also drawn
with corn pollen. It was east of the center halfway to the entrance
where we now stood. Going off on a line between the center and
the west were two arms, one going directly to the south and the
other arm going directly to the north. These arms were surely corn
pollen too. The line stopped in the west.

"Listen carefully," Agnes said. "Walk around to the south and
place one jar of water on the corn pollen circle, then go to the west
and there you will sit, but before you sit down go to the north.
Place the other jar of water on the corn pollen circle and return to
the west. Sit directly across from me—you in the west and me in
the east. Do you understand?"

"Yes, I think so. Can I ask what I'm doing?"

"The mound in the center is called Central Mountain. The path
of corn pollen is called the Lizard Trail. The crystal in the center is
male in character. You might call it a transmitter. We have to hurry
and catch the moment. Do what I tell you."

We entered the circle from the east. I put the jars of water on the
corn pollen circles in the south and north, and then sat down
directly across from Agnes in the west. Agnes extinguished the dim

candle, and in a moment the corn pollen shone in the dark. There was just enough light to be able to see and Agnes appeared as a grey-blue luminous form. From my perspective, the lines that shimmered in the very dim light looked roughly like the stick figure of a man.

Agnes set out three crystals on the ground. They were the size of a fist. She placed five on her left side, then she set out five similar crystals on the ground on her right side.

"These are helper crystals," Agnes said. "These helpers are friends of Crystal Woman."

Agnes proceeded to thrust six prayer sticks, three on each side of her, into the earth floor in front of each crystal. Now there was one jutting up in front of each helper crystal. Each stick had been wrapped with string and had feathers hanging from it.

"Lynn, you must sit perfectly still from this moment on. Night is the time of introspection. We will now begin to prepare to bring forth Crystal Woman. This is the favorable time."

We sat for several moments and then Agnes began to sing in Cree. I had never heard the song before and had no idea what the words meant. When she finished, she began to pray. Her arms were held up and her head was thrown back. I could see one star reflected in the crystal that sat between us. The star must have shone down and become visible from the smoke hole in the lodge. The longer I stared, the more it seemed to grow brighter.

Agnes withdrew a pouch that was underneath her Pendleton shirt and untied the thong. She dipped her finger into the substance that was in the bag and rubbed it in the middle of her forehead. She then touched the substance to her tongue.

At that moment, I realized she held a large crystal in her lap. She worked that crystal until it reflected the star glowing with a cold blue-white light from the central crystal. Agnes seemed to fall into a trance, and she didn't say anything for a long time. Her head had fallen forward, and she seemed to be fixated on the crystal in her lap. Finally, she turned her head up and looked at me. I was aware of a great deal of discomfort in my stomach—according to Agnes, this was the area of my will.

"Lynn, you fell from your path when you didn't cut the cords leading from you to your book. You are still attached by a spirit umbilical cord. These ropes must be broken. You are bound by your own doing. When you finished the book, you needed to separate from it. Like a child that separates from its parents, you need to go through a rite of passage. You must sign your book in blood and let her go on her own way. You accomplish this ceremonially by doing a giveaway. Do you consent to this?"

"Yes, but I don't know what to do."

There was a moment of silence. "I know you don't," she said. "I will guide you."

Again, Agnes's head slumped forward. She appeared to be unconscious. I wondered if I would ever be able to travel with her in a dream trance. I began to feel uncomfortable, my legs hurt, but I knew better than to move.

My eyes began to play tricks on me. The lines of corn pollen had a kind of dry, sharp glow that began to soften and blur. I thought of my book and her message and closed my eyes. I knew she was right. My stomach still hurt and I wanted to double over, but I managed to stay quiet.

Agnes had not told me what to do. Thrown back upon myself, I began to feel uneasy. I was not in touch with my body at all. My immobility began to make me dizzy. I was just about to move when Agnes spoke her prayers thanking the powers for coming. The ceremony was over.

Agnes gave me complicated instructions on how to clean up everything. As soon as I did the work, she said, "Come, let's sit outside for a while."

I got up and followed her out. My sense of reality had become distorted and confused. There was enough light beyond the buffalo hide to see, and my surroundings became suddenly more specific. We sat down and I tried to make myself comfortable.

"What happened during the ceremony, Agnes?" I asked. "You were far away."

"It is very difficult to explain. The substance I rubbed over my vision eye is red and comes from a teacher plant. I immediately touched it to my tongue. Without a word of warning, the herb leaps across from the plant world and journeys with me into the dream lodge. It takes many years to learn to handle this. It is not for everyone and it is not for you."

"Do you remember what you told me?"

"Of course I remember. That is my job to remember because I am a medicine woman."

"I thought you were in a trance state," I said.

"I was, but I was also conscious of everything that went on. I was taken to a place that is sacred to the grandparents. The first thing I did was call the four lizard spirits to help me hold onto Crystal Woman. They came right away to my call. Then I asked for help from my teacher plant. The crystal in my lap was feminine, and it was through her that I was able to glimpse another face of the form. My helper crystals also gave me power, and they became protective for a time. When everything was as it should be, I saw Crystal Woman come down. She is shaped like a woman and has all the colors of the rainbow. Crystal Woman jumped out of the crystal on Central Mountain and, like a whirling fiery light, came forward and stood on corn-pollen star. It is necessary to have corn-pollen star between me and the crystal on Central Mountain because Crystal Woman wishes to possess the seer. Her beauty is unimaginable. She glimmers like a million jewels. Her sound is very loud, like the cracking of whips. The only thing that stops Crystal Woman from taking me is the law that she cannot leave the corn-pollen star."

"What would happen if she possessed you, Agnes?"

"She would break me into a thousand jeweled pieces. I would shatter like glass caught up in worlds impossible to explain. In your tongue, I would be insane."

"What happens when Crystal Woman stands before you?" I asked.

"Crystal Woman has a star spirit. Do you remember I once told you that you can trap a spirit?"

"Yes."

"Do you know how noble Grandfather Sun is? All of the children of Grandfather Sun, the planets, revolve around him. A star is the same as Grandfather Sun. A star has a great and noble spirit, just like Grandfather Sun. Nothing would be alive without him. Using the crystal is like bringing the other reflection—the spirit world—into manifestation. There are four worlds. Three are material. The fourth has mastery over all other realms—it is called rainbow world.

"Crystal Woman told me how you left your path. The star spirit came down into the male crystal. She leaped onto the star. She told me just what was needed."

"You could actually hear her speak?"

"Yes, her voice is as beautiful as she herself."

"How does Crystal Woman know anything about me?"

"Crystal Woman has many aspects. As I said, star energy. The spirit of the water is accompanied by the lizards to the crystal on Central Mountain. Your fibers were also attached to the crystal on Central Mountain. And, last, it is the power of the teacher plant that braids each aspect together. Crystal Woman knew you from your fibers. Twirling out in front of you, your fibers held the spirit of something, but I didn't know what. Now I know it is the book you have written that must be plucked from you. I should have known, but it took a talk with Crystal Woman to make me understand."

"Well, what do I do now?"

"Tomorrow we will do a giveaway. You were uncomfortable during the ceremony. That's because you have given away some of your power. Women do this, and then feel alien in a situation. And your stomach hurts because your will has grown flabby. You have not been seeing with your body-mind—those eyes are just below your stomach. The ceremony will reestablish your relationship with Wakan—your life force. Tonight I am very tired. Meetings with Crystal Woman are very exhausting. She is very quick-witted and knows practically everything there is to know. I am going to bed."

The explanation Agnes gave me seemed complete. However, I did not know whether I should take her on a literal level or draw my own conclusions. One thing I knew for certain: her knowledge was vast. Her world became more mysterious all the time.

In the morning, we drove towards Agnes's cabin. She seemed exhilarated, and her mood was contagious. She told me to stop by the store in Crowley and buy several colors of ribbons.

Crowley was nearly deserted when we pulled up to the general store, except for some old men standing around the door. As I was selecting ribbon, a tiny white-haired Indian woman wearing a pink calico dress walked by, bent over and talking to herself. She suddenly lurched forward and tripped, dumping a stack of colored paper all over the floor.

"Here, let me help you." I quickly scooped up the papers and handed them back to her. She mumbled something under her breath that I couldn't understand. Her eyes darted furtively from side to side, like a weasel's. I thought to myself that she was behaving in a very odd manner. Her movements were almost childlike.

She grabbed the papers out of my hand, seeming to bow while shaking her head. She spun around and went over to the counter. The man behind the cash register said, "Well, Phoebe, will there be anything else today?"

Phoebe glanced suspiciously at me and then took out a small beaded bag and paid the cashier. She glanced at me again, saying something in Cree that I couldn't understand. She marched out of the store. The cashier smiled and shrugged his shoulders.

"Agnes," I said back in the car, "I'm curious about a woman I saw in the store. She has white hair pulled up in a topknot on her head, and she's about five feet tall. I think her name is Phoebe."

"Yes, I saw her come out."

"There is something peculiar about that woman. Do you have any idea what she does with all that construction paper?"

"Yes, I think I know what she does with it. It is part of her make-believe world. She cuts out dolls. Phoebe is around eighty years old. Most people think she's crazy, but I prefer to think she's complicated."

The old woman hadn't looked menacing, but I felt a knot of apprehension tighten in the back of my mind. We drove back to the cabin in silence and I dismissed Phoebe from my thoughts.

"What are the ribbons for?" I asked, as we walked down the path.

"For your giveaway. Red represents the south, white north, black west, and yellow for the east."

Agnes bustled around the cabin, opening the windows, hanging up some herbs she had collected and boiling water for coffee. She handed me an old shirt and told me to cut it up into six-inch squares.

"Where is your book? Put it on the table."

I got a copy of *Medicine Woman* from my things and placed it near my coffee cup. After the squares of cloth were cut, Agnes showed me how to make them into small pouches and to fill them with tobacco mixed with various other herbs. I tied each pouch with the colored ribbons. Then, after getting two of my feathers, we took the book and bundles out under a tree. Agnes spread out her medicine blanket and we sat on it across from each other. She took out her pipe and prayed to the four directions, the Great Spirit, and the powers of the universe and the Grandparents, and asked them to hear me in my giveaway. I smoked the pipe. Then Agnes cut a small piece of her hair and mine and we put that in a bundle, tying it with red ribbon.

She laughed. "That is in case I had any hold on your book," she said. "Give me your hand." Holding it, she pierced my finger with the sharp point of her hunting knife. I winced.

"Now smudge the front and back cover of your book with blood. Pray to release her from you and to let her grow now and find her own way. She is now separate from you. It is good." I laid the book back down and Agnes sang in Cree. Emotion welled up in me and I began to cry. I realized that I had felt something like a mother with her child. Agnes had me tie all the bundles to the feathers. After we had said our final words and rolled up the blanket, she told me to go up on the road to the crossroads and to tie the entire bundle to the branch of a tree where I would be sure someone would find and take it. It did not matter who took it, or if the spirit of the tree took it.

Soon it was done.

When I returned, the sun was shining and I felt better than I had in a long time. I joined Agnes for a walk. We went down to the creek and sat on the bank and shared some jerky. It was a lovely green site, and the water tumbled by and off into the distance. A flock of wild geese flew overhead.

"Look," I said, pointing.

"Yes. They are the keepers of the earthly dream."

"This seems like a dream here, compared to what I'm used to back in Los Angeles."

I was happy. It was the first time in several weeks I had felt completely safe. I knew that no matter what happened, Agnes would be there to help me. Absently, I began to throw stones into the rippling water of the creek.

"How do you know you should be throwing rocks into the creek? Perhaps you should be taking rocks out." Agnes's face appeared suddenly birdlike and her eyes sparkled. I knew she was having some fun at my expense. "I think you have just made a gift of two stones to the water. The water now tells me that you can take two stones out. The water also gives me permission to teach you a little about rock medicine."

"What should I do?" I asked, trying to get into the swing of Agnes's jolly attitude.

"Well, close your eyes, Lynn. Then reach in and pick a rock out of the stream and feel it and see if it belongs to you. It if does, hold it for awhile in the palm of your hand so it fits like this."

Agnes placed a small grey rock in her hand so it sat in her palm comfortably.

"Now go ahead and see if you can find something."

I closed my eyes and plunged my right hand into the creek and explored around for rocks. The water was freezing cold and my hand was quickly growing numb. After rejecting several, I felt a small rock that had several smooth sides. With my eyes still closed, I picked it up out of the water and held it. It felt rather like the shape I was looking for.

"Can I open my eyes, Agnes?"

"Yes, and keep them open. I want you to find another rock and reach in and get it."

I searched the gritty bottom. I laid claim to a black one that shimmered underneath the clear current.

"This one," I said, reaching for it.

"Now sit here in front of me and let me tell you something about your rocks. Hold the one you just selected in your left hand and move it around. The heel of your hand is the south. Every stone has seven faces. The first face is sound."

"Agnes, you're not going to tell me that rocks make a sound?"

"Yes, I am going to try to describe to you your great unawareness—and how you misinterpret and misunderstand the things around you. Rocks do indeed make a sound. All things that the Great Spirit has put here continually cry to be heard. The problem is, there are few who listen. I remember the first time I ever heard the rocks crying. It was a day very much like today. I was a girl like you—full of false pride. I longed to be anything other than what I thought myself to be. I belittled myself in my mind. I was young then, and I thought I was very tough. I wasn't the old woman you see here before you now.

"I won't try to explain the things going on in my heart in those days. I was very downcast. I had not made peace with wisdom. I walked one day into a great canyon. I sat on a boulder, not knowing then that it had called me. I watched the white foamy stream as it curved off into the mouth of the canyon. It was midday and I smoked one cigarette after another—examining the endless formations and random array of the rocks strewn about the canyon floor. I thought the water that rushed by was making its sound only for me.

"There was so much pain inside of me that day I believed a part of me was screaming and this was being drowned out by the rushing of the stream. When I let this feeling come into me, I was suddenly aware that the rocks sensed my pain and were crying with me. Don't imagine that I heard this sound by my ears alone—I heard it by my whole awareness. I ran all the way home to my mother. She was washing clothes.

" 'Mother,' I said. 'I heard the rocks crying. Could this be true?'

"My mother looked at me.

"My child, you are walking a path little-traveled these days—the path of a medicine woman. I know nothing of these things, but I have heard it said that rocks are a way to knowledge. Do not be

afraid, child. It is a good sign.' So you see, it was the beginning for
me and my long apprenticeship to the rocks. The rock in your hand
speaks to me and tells me many things."

"Agnes, did you know they're selling pet rocks in the city?"

She didn't seem interested. She said, "I already have too many
pet rocks and I just don't have room for any more."

I had to laugh—the irony of "pet rocks" had completely escaped
her.

"Do you think of your rocks as pets, Agnes?"

"Oh yes, but sometimes I wonder if they don't think of me as
their pet Indian. What is a pet but one who is friendly? I have had
many rocks that are quite ferocious. There have been some I could
not possibly conquer, some I would not dare offend. There have
been some that the responsibility of holding was too great."

"So then you are telling me that all rocks make sound?"

"Not at all. Some rocks are silent. You have to coax them to
speak."

"Will you tell me some of the other faces of a rock?"

"As I said, there are seven. The second face is sight."

I looked at Agnes in a state of bewilderment.

"I am saying that rocks can see you. Any rock can. The eyes of a
rock are more difficult to explain than rock talk. For now, I will say
that rocks are in the mind of the great spirit. The great spirit sees
within you and me, and the great spirit sees from within the rock.
There is one difference. Many rocks can see a long way off, like a
crystal. If you see something happening in the crystal a long way
away or even in the future, it wasn't you who saw it. It was the
crystal, and you saw what the crystal saw. More correctly, the eyes
of the crystal saw it. The eyes of a rock are a thousand times better
than yours or mine. Rocks had to develop that power. You can
learn from most stones. Many rocks come from other worlds. Like
meteors do. With them you can see the children of the stars. Many
of those meteorites are lost and want to go home. If you comfort
them, they will show you brilliant worlds where few dare go.

"If you had eyes like the stones, you could explore the universe and both the future and the past. Yes, you could go back into ancient times. If I were to tell you that the stones have seen all of knowledge, to you it would sound absurd. Yet that is true, and they are waiting to reveal their secrets. There are rocks that have eyes that can show you treasures more precious than anything you've ever seen."

"And can you see with the eyes of a rock, Agnes?"

"Yes. Anyone can, but it is very difficult to describe. You first see a cold mist or fog. Then you capture a glimpse. You have to seize that glimpse and stop it and then you can see what the rock sees. Some rocks are very deceitful and will try to play tricks on you. You know this by the colors of what they show you. If the colors are too perfect, then you know it is part of their dream. But if you see ordinary colors, you will know they are trying to tell you something you should know. Sometimes rocks will show you painful things that you will not wish to see. Other times they will simply show you what is about to happen."

I bounced the rock around in my hand. It was beginning to feel more like a crystal ball than a rock. My mind was teeming with so many questions that I didn't know which of them to ask.

"I want to learn to see with the stones, Agnes."

"Rocks have no problem seeing. You do. Rocks are very slow and have sat around since the beginning, developing the powers we are speaking of. Truly, within all rocks, there is an eye. The laws that govern it do not restrict it to immediate boundaries. The eyes of a rock can skip out anywhere. They can provide a gateway to the sacred maze, what medicine people call the crystal world, where they go to find the answers to things. You can learn to go into those gateways. Rocks can show what you are going to become. They can show you lost and forgotten things. They can show you who stole something and what they did with it. It is the eye of the rock that will show you."

"What are some other faces?"

"The third face is scent. Not many humans can smell worth a darn, but believe me, rocks can catch scents that were around a hundred years ago. Rocks can smell the most subtle and delicate fragrance."

"I suppose you are going to tell me there is a nose in a rock."

Agnes laughed. "No, not exactly. Rock is a nose. Stalking has to do with scent. The old trackers who lost the trail knew who to ask. They asked the stones if they had scented their prey, and the stones pointed them off in the right direction. This was due to the stones' ability to smell. The stone you are holding smells you and and will remember you for a millenium. That stone would recognize you no matter what tricks you played or how you tried to hide yourself. When I am looking for someone, I take a stone who knows the person. The stone smells the person out and I never miss finding them. None of us can ever hope to develop our ability to smell to the degree of a rock. It is a good idea, however, to know how talented they are."

"What is the fourth face, Agnes?"

"Taste."

"You are going to tell me rocks are real gourmets, right?"

"Yes, but I can see I am going much too fast for you. You have limitations that will take time to erase. Yes, a rock can eat. That is a face. The fifth face is touch. A rock has the ability to feel. The sixth face is emotion. A rock is emotional and has the ability to cause emotion in others. The seventh face is awareness. I have already said that the great spirit is contained in a rock. Rocks are like people and have varying degrees of self-awareness. Rocks are like all other living things. It's just they are of a denser quality."

"Here, let me show you a different medicine wheel. As you know, there are many wheels."

Agnes smoothed an area of flat ground and took a stick and drew a large circle. She then drew twelve spokes, explaining what each represented. They were areas of internal learning such as love, sharing, and healing. Each spoke had a corresponding color.

"Give my your stones, Lynn."

I handed them to her.

"Now watch," she said. "Remember, I told you the heel of the palm of your hand was the south? This stone will go in this wheel exactly the way it was in the palm of your hand. When you hand someone a stone or anything else, there is a meaning to it. When you pick up a stone and hold it, there is great meaning. One day you will be able to read things like this without the help of the wheel, but for now we will use it."

Agnes placed the rock in the center of the circle and started to read it. "Both of your rocks are black. Black stands for learning and seeking the light. You see now that it is proper for you to work from the West—from dreaming and introspection. The angles show me that your goals are healing and creativity. Purple is a very good color for you to have near you at all times. One day you will work with crystals. Look—it's interesting that both of your rocks have five angles."

Agnes demonstrated this by showing me that each stone could rest on five different sides without falling or moving.

"You see," she went on, "this refers again to creativity. Five is the number of the human and the number of the hands. You have five fingers. This tells me your power will come from your work of looking within and dreaming.

"One day I will teach you how to use the stones for personal power. Before you can work with crystals, you have to learn to work with the rocks. A personal stone contains the memory of the universe and should be carried in a pouch. A pouch is a sort of void, a womb. Just as the universe is contained in the void, you should keep your personal rocks in a pouch."

Agnes began untying a bundle.

"What are we going to do now?" I asked.

The bundle contained various pieces of cloth and pieces of hide. Agnes selected a piece of doe hide. She laid out various instruments, knives, and scissors.

"Let me show you."

She instructed me to cut a circle and also a thong out of the doeskin. I took the scissors and in a few minutes I was finished.

"Now punch twelve holes to finish your medicine wheel. Remember the wheel stands for balance in spirit."

I went around the doeskin circle punching with an awl.

"Now thread it with your thong. Good. These are your first personal stones. Each will go in its own sacred pouch of wisdom."

I repeated the process and made another pouch. This time I was a little more skilled. Agnes nodded approvingly as I worked, and for a time after I was finished, she stared at me rigidly.

"Did I do it right?" I asked.

Agnes examined it and handed it back to me. She looked at me. She seemed to be struggling for the right words.

"There is much to teach. I was just thinking, these are your first personal stones. Carry them with you in your pouch along with a feather for your higher self lodge and principles to live by. Put in a seed and a kernel of corn. Wait until the corn comes to you. You might find it while making dinner. You might find it on the ground. Put in a helper herb—herb that helps cure any deficiency you might have—sage would be good."

Agnes explored around in her bundle and got two twigs of sage. She handed them to me.

"Put these in your pouch."

She found two pieces of eagle down.

"These should go in your pouch."

I took them and stuffed them into the pouches with the rocks and sage.

"Whether you know it or not, I have been telling you about birth. Birth was when the stones walked out of the earth. Other sacred fires were here before us. The stones are the keepers of the hills. The secrets of the ages are written on the stones from the dawn of birth. Stones are universally used for tools, weapons, rituals, fire beds, medicine stones. Mother Earth was once stone. Now we look around for the pieces."

"Are you saying that we were once actually stone?"

"Yes. I will tell you of a ceremony. When a new child comes to the people, I search for a little white stone with a natural hole in it. Stones with natural holes have a beautiful medicine spirit. They are extremely powerful, even tiny ones. When we find one of those white stones with a hole in it, we make a pouch and put the hair of

a porcupine or moose in it. Then we put in the stone. And last we
tie it around the baby's wrist. It is a gift from mother earth to the
infant. That tiny stone contains the wisdom of the ages. It is the
child's first personal stone and there is much thanksgiving among the
people. Now let's go make supper. Ruby is coming over."

I was suddenly filled with apprehension at the thought of seeing
Ruby. Thoughts of Red Dog—my reason for learning of new worlds
and ways of seeing—flooded into my mind in a terrible rush. We
walked quickly back to the cabin. My fingers hurt from clutching
the stone pouches so tightly.

An hour later Agnes, Ruby, and I were seated in silence around
Agnes's table. It did not seem like the right time to ask Ruby for
anything. She kept turning her head and looking at the front door as
though she were expecting someone. She smoked one cigarette after
another, and when she was finished, she ground the butts out on
the floor—a nice mess for me to clean up. If she was trying to
irritate me, she was doing a good job.

Agnes gathered up the dishes and took them to the sink. She
rolled up the sleeves of her Pendleton shirt and began washing
them. Doing dishes was usually my job, and I wondered why Agnes
was doing them.

Ruby reached over and patted my knee. "Lynn, your acts were
courageous and right," she said. "It was risky."

"What was risky?" I blurted.

"It was risky to pit an idiot like you against Red Dog."

Agnes came over and set out three paper cups of tea in front of
us.

"Agnes," Ruby said, "something has to be done about the danger
Lynn is in. Red Dog could come busting in here any second. Lynn
doesn't know how to hold her space. The time for dreaming is over.
Now is a time to act. I am glad you are here, but I'm afraid I can't
help you."

"What do you mean you can't help me? You have to help me!"

I handed Ruby two packs of cigarettes. She laughed and shoved
them back across the table at me.

"I don't smoke that brand. I have no use for your cigarettes."

I looked anxiously at Agnes, trying to divine what I should do. I tried to say something, but Ruby waved her hand for me to be silent. She took the paper cup and turned her back for a moment. I wondered what she could be doing. When she handed the cup back to me, hot tea spurted out in all directions. I yelped and leapt from my chair, throwing the cup in the sink. Agnes and Ruby were laughing and slapping their legs, and I gawked at them incredulously.

Ruby said, "You're like that cup, Lynn. You're full of holes."

Again I looked to Agnes for some kind of assurance. Her black eyes shone ominously. "Ruby is right, Lynn." She pointed at my midsection. "There, there, and there—all over."

"You're fooling me—both of you. You're trying to frighten me again. I don't believe you."

"Think what you want, but you're like a sieve," Ruby said. "Your power is leaking out of you, pouring out. You are getting ever weaker. You have no protection at all. You are open and inviting trouble by your attitude. All manner of things could hurt you right now."

"You are attracting influences like moths to a flame," Agnes said. "You must be very careful because you are in a dangerous place."

"I thought my acts protected me."

Agnes and Ruby looked at one another and then looked back at my expectant face. I don't know what the actual psychological process was, but I knew what they were telling me was true. I became aware for a fleeting instant of clusters of holes floating around within me. The strange way I had been feeling began to make some sense.

"I think I understand. What should I do to protect myself?"

"Lynn, you're my apprentice and it is law that I must help you. You must learn to be a woman of ability, and by that I mean you must know how to protect yourself from Red Dog. You must make a decision to learn to help yourself. You must learn to make medicine shields."

"What kind of shields are you talking about?"

"There are as many shields as there are dangers to be shielded from. Right now you have to learn to shield the disappearances in your spirit body."

"Why am I suddenly in such great danger?"

"You've always been like that, but now you are attractive because now you have more knowledge."

"How many shields must I make?"

"For adequate protection," Ruby said, "you must make five shields. That is the number for the warrioress human."

"What do I have to learn?"

Ruby took a sip of tea. "Everything. You have to learn everything. If you can make the shields and learn their meaning, you can know the sacred law belt and find your sisters."

"What is the sacred law belt and who are my sisters?"

"You will learn of all this much later," Ruby said. "Most people protect themselves by nature; they don't know about trust. You trust and you must learn about protection."

"For now, Lynn," Agnes said, "you are going to have to learn how to focus protective energy. This is part of shield-making."

Ruby shook her head disgustedly. Her hands gripped the edge of the table. Both of them leaned over me. I took a deep breath. It was some kind of examination.

"What are you doing?" I asked.

Ruby was running her hand over me again, about six inches from my body.

Ruby shook her head negatively. "Still lots of holes."

Outside the cabin I could hear the wind surging through the trees. I could see leafy tree branches through the window. Holes in my body—the whole thing seemed incredible. Ruby began to chuckle and then sobered up.

"In the old days," Agnes said, "women made all the shields. Then everything got confused and men became the artisans. To make a shield in the proper manner, you have to destroy the conflicting parts of yourself. A shield is protective medicine. It is also a mirror. There are shields for practically everything. There are shields with so much power they will bring victory in battle. There are shields that will give you courage. There are shields that protect you from a sorcerer's attack. There are shields that bring the allies in time of need. But remember that an ally can't fight for you—only with you. There are truth shields, and if you hold up that power no one can lie to you. Shields are not only for defense. They stand as a record of who you are in the world in all your aspects—mental, emotional, physical, and spiritual. They stand for your sacredness within. They can be placed outside the lodges to tell people who you are."

Ruby lit a cigarette and pushed her chair back. She looked as though she was waiting for me to say something. She blew a puff of smoke toward the ceiling and rolled the cigarette back and forth in her fingers.

"Lynn," she began, "English words are sometimes unfamiliar to me, but I would like to tell you a story. My people say that a warrior named Mountain Lake wanted to make a shield. Mountain Lake went to the shield-maker women and asked them to help him. 'I will do many giveaways and go on a vision quest. I will trade anything. I want a shield that has every power in it.' 'That is not possible,' the shield-maker women said. 'That is the shield you already have, but it is not woken up. We think it unwise of you to seek these powers before your time.' The warrior insisted. 'I want to be the most powerful warrior,' Mountain Lake said. 'Honor me with a shield that contains all power.' The shield-maker women had a ceremony and talked all during the night arguing about what to do. The next day the warrior again came to them. 'We have agreed among ourselves,' they said. 'We will make you a shield with all power in it. Your good deeds are well known and we will honor you in this fashion.' Mountain Lake went away and did his vision quest and told the women what he saw. Then he waited for his shield to be made.

"Talk went around the village that the shield-maker women were making the warrior a shield with all power and the power of completion in it. When the shield was finished, the women called the man to them. Three friends came with him. 'We have done as you bid us,' the shield-maker women said, and the shield was woken up in ceremony.

"The warrior looked at the shield proudly. The symbols from his vision quest were beautifully executed. He put it on his arm and held it in an attitude of defense. When he did this, he suddenly burst into flames. In moments, all that was left of the warrior were his ashes. Since that time, a shield with total personal power has been called a sacrifice or the gateway shield. Now shields are prepared for special purposes. Shield-making is a serious and sacred business."

"Is bursting into flames what I have to look forward to?"

"Lynn, I will show you what you have to look forward to," Agnes said. She moved across the cabin and knelt down by her bed. She fished around underneath it and pulled out a circular bundle. The bundle was composed of various animal skins. She put it on the bed and unlaced the rawhide.

"It is an ancient medicine shield," Agnes said.

The shield was breathtaking. It looked enormous in the tiny cabin. The disk shape practically covered the entire bed. Several sets of hawk feathers hung from the bottom rim. It seemed to be impregnated with a natural force. It excited me, and for a moment I forgot everything and was lost in its beauty.

"It's easily the most beautiful shield I've ever seen," I said.

"I like it, too," Ruby said, edging closer.

"Hands off, Ruby," Agnes said. "I know you'd love to get your talons on it."

Ruby turned away in a huff.

"Look here," Agnes said. Out of the pocket that was hidden under the top rim, Agnes pulled out a yellowed lace handkerchief. It looked so old I thought it might flake apart. "This shield belonged to my grandmother," Agnes explained. "And this handkerchief was traded to her in 1893 by the Governor General's wife."

"Good medicine," Ruby said, gently touching the lace. "Strong."

"Agnes, thank you for showing me," I said. 'Ruby, can you make shields like this one?"

"Not exactly like that. That shield could be a great friend to a medicine person. It's not the kind of shield you would use. You are an apprentice and you are at the beginning. I'm not sure if you know anything. This is a female shield. Some shields are half male and half female—in balance. Some are male alone. All shields are for the individual. The great shield, the medicine wheel, is for all the people.

"An ideal shield for you would be a balanced shield, the kind of shield that will bring knowledge and reflect the particular things you will need to know and work with. Your first shield will have to be a shield that has strong water medicine or a spirit shield. Do you know of turtle medicine?"

"No, what is that?" I asked.

Agnes answered. "A turtle is representative of mother earth, but she carries the great shields on her back—she is the keeper of the knowledge of the spirit clans that are scattered over the earth; some spirit clans are visible and some are invisible. Everyone belongs to one of those spirit clans.

"There is a problem. You have to recognize your spirit clan, and that's not so easy. An act of power is required. If you do an act of power, you'll be tested by one spirit clan. If you're lucky, that will be the one for you. Chances are you'll be tested for nothing. When you meet the test, you must stand motionless. Throw your shoulders back and be proud of what you've accomplished. Let the representative of the spirit clan test you and, whatever you do, don't run away in terror."

"What happens if you find your spirit clan?" I asked.

"Then you can be one of the invisible ones. You can have true power. Anything and everything will be at your command. Whatever you want, you can have it."

"How did these spirit clans begin?"

"They began in ancient time. You see, now is not the only time the human was teetering on the brink of disaster. Mankind is heading toward cataclysm. In those ancient times there was power like the sun—powers that would make the atomic bomb look like a firecracker. There was a war on mother earth, the likes of which has never been seen before or since. The people who were left made up

their minds that such a monstrous war was never going to happen
again. Spirit clans were formed to contain all knowledge. Half of the
spirit clans are visible, and half of them are invisible."

"And you say that I belong to one of these clans?"

"You certainly do. Everyone on mother earth belongs to a spirit
clan. The problem is that you have to find it. They don't know who
you are. You don't know who they are. It's a little like walking
around in the dark.

"Making your shields will help you in this search," Agnes went
on. "When you make a shield, you must be united in yourself.
With each shield you will cross over to a quality that dwells in you
apart from your usual opinions of being. This quality can then be
infused with light. Each of us is like a piece of the great smoking
mirror, all reflecting the same light.

"Your shields are like paintings. When you have a true vision,
there can be no doubt that you walk in that vision. Your shield
designs will be the hatching of your vision. We call it the floating
egg within the dreaming. The floating egg must be taken to the nest,
and that nest is your shield.

"It takes great skill to construct the shield properly. There is the
story of Painted Face. 'I have lost my face,' she told her
grandmother. 'You haven't lost anything—you have lost your
painting.' 'What must I do, grandmother?' 'You must learn to see
yourself within the shattered smoking mirror that is illusion.' Painted
Face then set to work through life experiences and visions, fitting
the broken pieces of the great smoking mirror together like a puzzle.
When she was finished, she knew who she was. She was Painted
Face.

"It is my responsibility as your medicine teacher to give you
ability—the ability to fit the broken pieces of the great smoking
mirror back together. You will discover that the mirror is actually
four mirrors—Four Mirrors was a great teacher like your Jesus, and
they say that even his sacred name dissolves the lie. As you develop
your will, you will begin to understand the inner and outer aspects
of these designs and you will begin to pull them in from the rim of
your vision to the center of yourself—the joining of the wolf roads.

You will one day be able, with the focus of your attention, to set down your personal shields and use the great medicine represented in each of them. You will be able to see how these wonderful powers bind together and how they belong to you.

"Lynn, you often bounce from one direction to another like a rubber ball, hit by forces that wish to control you. In your world, these forces could be political or social or whatever; but they are all forms of sorcery. That is why it is important for you to construct four directions. You need to be able to work in every direction, although your place on the great wheel is in the north."

"I thought you said I have to construct *five* shields?"

"A medicine person has five faces. First is the face of the council. Second is the face of food or diet. Third is the face of history. Fourth is the face of wisdom. And fifth is the face of the teacher. These are within the four. You see, you are the fifth shield. North is where you experience wisdom. It will be the easiest shield for you because you are already close to that power. Your totem is she buffalo. North, then, is your centering tree."

"Not all the warriors and warrioresses have to work with five shields. For some there are no shields at all and no discovery. There is no initiation for them. There is no dance, no song."

Ruby stopped talking and nodded her head. She had taken the packages of cigarettes and was rubbing them over the table slowly. I wondered if there was some significance to her action. She said, "Look at the marriages. Marriage is a powerful medicine. Sometimes it can get confused. A man may say, 'My wife is a star. I am the pilot. I am producing for her.'"

"A woman can destroy a man by her body, language, and thoughts. But in destroying him, she destroys herself. She gives over to his intelligence. She says, 'My identity is linked with him, my husband.' But her dream should have it's own identity. There are many lessons in attachment. But what right do we have to hold on?

"Some day, all the medicine shields will go away. The medicine shields are linking up to form a grid over the mother earth to help during the cleansing.

"Each person has her own medicine. Honor each person and salute the medicine shield within her.

"In our world, we form a hand—five medicine women or five medicine men. With the hand you have the numbers, life, unity, equality, eternity, teacher. They add up to perfection. In women's councils we change positions so each person experiences these other positions and can become a total person—there is growth in change.

"You are still learning the way. One day soon you will understand the meaning of the sisterhood of the shields. I cannot explain it to you any better. Simply realize that in your earth-walk, each shield belongs to a larger single shield. You have to become a master of the shields and, when you do, you will discover the warrioress's destiny."

Smoke hung in the air all around Ruby. She was chain-smoking continually as she talked. Agnes was watching all the while, seemingly on the verge of saying something; but she didn't interrupt. Ruby had spoken to me, choosing her words very carefully so that I could understand her heavily accented English. I had never heard her speak at such length or so profoundly. I was stunned at how well she knew me—certainly, in some ways, better than I knew myself. I reached over and dropped the cigarettes that she had refused earlier back into her lap. She picked them up and this time she held them to her heart, then she put them on the table.

"Whew, I earned them," she said. For a second she smiled in my direction. It was all too brief. She sat stiffly and proudly. She said, "Lynn, I will help you with your journey into shield-balance. I will assist you mainly through Agnes because you are her apprentice. Her spirit is different from mine. You need someone who is much more tolerant and gentle than I am. Naturally, I serve a different purpose for you. I hang around to feed your fear."

"What do you mean?" I didn't like the sound of that.

Ruby sat partially obscured in the growing night shadows of the cabin. I was alert. Her eyes suddenly shone at me like the blue eyes of a Siberian husky. I was becoming uncomfortable—her gaze was producing a warm sensation around my navel.

"You see all of your own doubts in me," Ruby said. "You see your anger. You see many things that you don't like, even your own blindness. You don't like to be around me very much because you fear me. There will come a time when you will accept yourself in your totality and you will become indifferent to me. I will no longer be a threat to you. You will also become indifferent to Agnes. Right now you are not capable of that. You are not aware yet. But take a look at the contrary—the sacred clown who tests all your beliefs. When you have let loose of your fears to let them flutter off of their own accord, you will remember that the ancient way of strength is feminine, of the womb. It is receptive. You can hold up the shields and become self-reliant. When you become indifferent to me, your fear will have flown away. That will be a big medicine time for you. There will then be room for others. So now Agnes and I will talk over your shield path. You go outside and chop some wood."

The old crazy glint was back in Ruby's eyes. The first time I ever saw her she was standing on her porch brandishing a butcher knife. I thought she was going to chop me up in little pieces. Since that meeting, I have never known what to say to her.

I left the cabin as she told me to do. Outside, I tripped over a log that had been dropped on the steps. Agnes and Ruby laughed, and Agnes got up and closed the door. It was getting very dark. Above me lay a blanket of stars that lit up the sky. A new gold moon hung over the tops of the pine trees. The wind had died down. I had had a great talk with my teachers, and I was exhilarated. Ruby was right. She reflected all my fears, and I hated looking at them.

I lit the lantern and it sputtered as the flame took hold. I grabbed the axe and began splitting a couple of small logs. An owl hooted in the tree directly above me. I stopped chopping and put the axe against the woodpile. She hooted again. I took a few steps back from the tree and stared up into the branches. I could see her standing on a limb looking down at me with glassy eyes—eyes not unlike Ruby's.

I thought about the many Native Americans who fear and distrust the owl. Agnes said that it was an omen of change to see an owl nearby, and to me change had always been welcome. I was glad that I trusted the owl and considered it my friend. I reached into the pocket of my jeans and found some of my giveaway tobacco. I sprinkled some under the tree.

"This is for you," I said to the owl.

I went back to work, my muscles complaining from the unaccustomed exercise. At least an hour passed before the door to the cabin opened, throwing out a shaft of light. Ruby and Agnes emerged with their arms around one another. Just as they did, the owl hooted above me once more.

For a while, they stood on the porch chattering in Cree. First Agnes would laugh hilariously and then Ruby did the same. I continued with my chopping. They watched me for a time and then Ruby poked Agnes with her elbow.

Ruby walked toward me and stopped, rotating her head right and left as she pretended to check to make sure no one was about. Then she leaned over towards me and whispered ominously, "Lynn, you really don't stand much of a chance out here."

"What do you mean?"

She was gone so quickly into the dark that I wondered if she hadn't disappeared.

I called after her. "Ruby, don't you want me to drive you home?" But she was gone. An old blind lady on a nine-mile trek back to her own cabin.

"Does she always refuse to ride in cars?" I asked Agnes.

Agnes chuckled. "Only when she's in a hurry." We went back inside the cabin.

Agnes seemed mirthful. She was rummaging around in her chest of drawers. She didn't seem to be paying any attention to me. "Don't worry," she said. "We have much work to do. Tomorrow we will begin to construct your first shield."

She put some bundles of hide and other things on the table—an awl, scissors, knives, a length of twisted thong, and last, from under the bed, a long, bent sapling. Agnes had wedged the two ends of the sapling into a short piece of drain pipe, so that instead of being straight, it was curved. I watched her as she forced the two ends together into a three-foot circle. She did all this neatly after a few whittles with the knife; and then, using the thong, she tied it. Now it was a perfect hoop that she held up for my inspection.

Agnes looked at me seriously. "You must do it next time. Try and remember what I did."

"I will," I acknowledged, impressed with her abilities.

Presently, we went to bed. I lay quietly in the dark, trying to understand the meaning of my new shield path. I was excited and it was sometime before I fell asleep.

The following day I prepared the hides and stretched them onto the bent wood circle. It required such intense concentration that before I knew it, it was dinner time. Agnes had been inside the cabin sewing while I worked on the porch. I ate the game stew and biscuits ravenously.

After dinner, Agnes tipped her chair back against the wall and we sat without talking for awhile. The way she looked at me made me feel uncomfortable. Her eyes explored my face.

"Before you make your first shield, there are some things you need to know.

"First, only women can make their own shields. A man never can. It would be disastrous. A man can make another man's shield, but never his own. In the old way, a warrior would have a vision or a sign to know who was to make it for him, and a shield could never be made without the help of a woman. Women were the masters of the shield. Like I said, shields were either male or female in character. Balanced shields were half-female and half-male. This was done with energy. The things used to make the shield were of either male or female themselves."

"Can you give me an example."

"Sure. For instance, with color. Blue and green are male, and orange and pink are female. Certain pelts are male, and others are female. Finally, these energies are awakened."

"How is this done?"

"You awaken the shield by praying to the galaxy, the Milky Way. Pray to endless space. Pray to the sun. Pray to the seven: Earth. Jupiter. Mars. Neptune. Mercury. Moon. Venus. When you pray, put the galaxy into the shield. You ask for the medicine you want. Protect me from being shot. Protect me from disease. Ask the little bird Mercury to protect you from harm. Ask her for swiftness of mind and body. Ask the Sun and Jupiter to protect you from mass insanity. A feminine shield has the qualities of time and space. A feminine shield gives the warrior courage.

"I am speaking in your language now. In my own language, the words are better. Ask Mars for strength. Ask Mother Earth for charisma and healing. Pray to the moon for imagination and intuition. Another way to say this is 'The Seven Spirit Keepers of the Great Dream.' Pray to Sweet Medicine, animal things. Do we not appear again because of the animals? Pray to White Buffalo Woman for healing. She is the keeper of the plant world. Do we not appear again because of the plants?

"Some shields are purified under stones to give them power. Others are buried for a period of time under trees or under the Mother Earth.

"Medicine people see the different kinds of medicines in shields. You see a shield's real color and power. You can't eat this power. You can't steal it unless you know how. You can't burn it. The energy will still exist.

"There are many ways to make shields. I like to make them out of willow. You make a willow hoop, then you cut the rawhide in a circle. You stretch that over the willow form. You can use deerskin. Sometimes you see turtle shell cut in pyramids with a brass trade bead through the shell in a circle. Or you can braid horsehair on the rim of the shield with four white feathers. Horse bone etched with every kind of serpent is pretty. Or paint suns between horse bones."

"Are there any certain names for the various parts of the shields?" I asked.

"Yes, the undershield is called the blessing shield, the main body. The top shield is called his or her name or top picture or image. The whole shield is known as protection. There are names for various designs. Often male and female pyramids can be seen in the design of a shield. Colors have meaning, as I have said. White, for instance, is either male or female depending on how you push the color. White and red mixed together is more female. East, in the old way, was red; but red is now in the south. Gold is for the sun beings. Gold is east."

"Can you tell me about my first shield?"

"The most important thing to remember is that anything that is on a shield is there for a reason. It has special power and meaning for the carrier of the shield. A symbol is the picture of an idea. The idea comes from dreams or visions. The shield is the heart of a warrioress. The heart is the force that binds all things in this world together." Agnes reached over and gently touched the back of my hand. "Come, let's get some sleep."

When I woke up, Agnes was busy grinding dried herbs into a fine powder between two flat rocks.

I washed, combed out my hair, and dressed. When I was finished I sat down and watched. She dumped the mound of powder into a jar of water and shook it.

"What are you doing?" I asked.

"For you," she said. "One learns from watching the gnawers. I call it chipmunk water." She handed the jar to me. "Drink it."

I unscrewed the lid and sniffed. "It doesn't smell that good, Agnes."

"It is to give you strength, to rebuild you. It is the plant way you need. Drink," she said.

"Okay, Mom, I'll eat my spinach."

I drank the concoction down. It had a vaguely bitter taste, but I knew instantly that my body craved it.

"You need more time outdoors and more of the shining power of Grandfather Sun. You need strong muscles. Let your footsteps fall gently on the earth. Acknowledge power like a true sister. Listen carefully to your inner voice. We have much to do and only a little while to do it in. We need the sun."

Agnes stood up. She rummaged around the cabin and got several things. "Bring the hoop," she said pointing. "Come with me."

I followed her outside. She was carrying some sharp sticks and a bundle of leather. We didn't go far. Agnes motioned for me to sit down on the ground. "Put the hoop there between us."

We were then sitting across from one another at the crest of a small hill. Little birds were chirping, and I felt surrounded by life. After a while, Agnes spoke.

"Lynn, long ago I went to an important meeting of the Red Lodge Society. Only women were allowed. It took me several weeks to journey there with some other women. The lodges stood in a beautiful spot high in the mountains. We arrived on a peaceful day in late spring when the mountain bees and butterflies were all around. Outside the lodges stood the four great Red Lodge shields, and it was my joy to see them placed and ready for the renewals.

"In the Red Lodges there was much straight talk. We passed the talking stick among the women who were there. Many hearts were opened to the Great Spirit. All the Red Lodges had power. We all learned from each other and traded medicines. I noticed in one meeting that there was a shield hanging inside the lodge with long yellow hair on it—a human scalp. I realized it was a shield with great power, but for the life of me I could not decipher the hidden meaning. I was at a loss. This long yellow hair shield was very masculine, and yet it was made in such a way that the masculine could only increase the overall femininity of it. I shook my head in wonder.

"I asked my sister what she thought the proper meaning of the shield might be. She also shook her head in wonder. After the meeting was over, I went to the chief elder. I asked, 'Grandmother, what is the medicine of this puzzling shield?' She looked at me with kindness. 'That shield is called Destroyer-of-Children. It is a good shield, a shield with much dignity and meaning. Whenever a man kills the child within himself and hates his deadness and begins to treat innocent children harmfully, it is very bad medicine. The first law, my daughter, is that all power comes from woman. The second law is never to do anything that harms children. Are not children the center of the first shield? Always protect the children. The lesson of this shield is that many scalps will be taken from people who have harmed children.'

" 'Where does this scalp come from, grandmother?' I asked. The old woman spoke with sadness. 'As you know, my child, it was not long ago that it was the responsibility for a warrioress to challenge, fight, and honorably destroy one who would harm children. That long yellow hair is the scalp of a white soldier who was shooting and killing children he found hiding in the bushes down south. The soldier was enjoying himself. Shield Woman, who had already killed two other hunters, threw a hatchet in his chest. She took his scalp with his eyes wide open. I think he was surprised to be counted on by a woman.'

"After speaking with the grandmother, I left and went home. I thought about this shield for a long time. Today the world has changed, but the principles of this mighty law should be honored by everyone. When you discern a person, ask yourself the question, does this person honor the child within—for then he honors the child in the world."

"Agnes, that's an incredible story, one that I will always remember. There is so much harm done to children in the world today. What makes a man or a woman a child abuser?"

"A man has a womb, just like a woman. Many women are not sisters and have not developed their womb, and many men have not developed their womb. When a person's womb is not alive, there is no understanding of its fruit. These people interfere with a child's self-realization. They perpetuate the endless dream."

I nodded my head in agreement and her sharp, clear eyes focused on me.

"Lynn, you are at the beginning. I, as your teacher and advisor, am at the beginning also. All life and the life of a medicine woman is at the beginning. One day you will come to see this. Your way is born here." Agnes placed her fist over her heart. "Here is the light that came out of darkness. Here dwells the secrets that are like good food that will nourish you. Here is where words are born, words capable of giving you the great lie and the great truth."

Agnes picked up the willow hoop and held it up in front of me. "This hoop will become your first shield. It will be a very good and useful tool when you are finished. This shield begins at the beginning in the south, in the water. Look and try to see what lies ahead, for there are smells and things that grow that are giving signs. There are chokecherries with eyes like sapphires. In the old way, this was called Woman-of-Muddy-River Shield, the woman's blood shield."

"Is it also a child shield?" I asked.

"Yes, we have said it is Destroyer-of-Children shield. It is the shield of the silent ones. It is a spirit-way shield."

"My first shield will have many meanings," I said.

"Many," Agnes emphasized. She put the willow hoop down on the ground once more and pointed to the bottom rim closest to me. "The sacred altar will be there, in the south of your shield. Here are the teachings of the great rounds. Vegetation grows there also—the sacred teacher plants. Tobacco was the first."

Agnes moved her hand to the left and pointed. I realized she was addressing the left side of the hoop. "This part of your shield teaches of your body and your heart. It is the knowledge of plant medicines and poisons. The medicine pipe is here and the healing gourd. Plant balance is here and shield painting.

"Up here on your shield," Agnes continued, pointing at the area of the hoop closest to her, the part I recognized as north, "is the art of traveling and hearing at a distance. It is seven-waters dancing. It is working with crystals and learning of the crystals of the great wheel. In the center is the shaman tree, the medicine woman you will one day become."

Agnes and I talked at length about the various meanings of the directions of the south shield. She then began to instruct me in the actual art of making a shield. This aspect of shield-making, though it was an important aspect, indeed seemed secondary to the teachings she was endeavoring to impart.

"It is vital," Agnes said, "that you attend to every last detail in the exact way I tell you. Proper alignment of self is what we are seeking. If you can manage it, all other forms will follow."

For the next two days I prepared a deer hide as Agnes instructed me. I confined my activity to a level, grassy area not far from the cabin. Agnes appeared now and again to give instructions and to observe the process. She came and sat cross-legged when I was nearly finished, running her hand over the hide.

"Yes. You must become as soft as this deer hide is soft. This hide is not the hide of a war shield. This is your south shield hide and it requires softness."

"How do I become soft like this hide?" I asked.

"Our bodies have natural shields, but this is a problem. We lose our fluidity. When you are fluid and you fall down in a hole, it won't hurt you. If you are rigid, you will break your neck. I want you to take the shields out of your body and hold them in front of you. I want you to be fluid. Fluidity is a great power of the warrioress. Your first shield is a happy time, a celebration. Fluidity will let you go the way that is most natural. Fluidity lets you be yourself."

Late that afternoon I was stretching and fitting the hide around the willow hoop. Agnes came once more and sat across from me. She smiled from time to time at my fumbling attempts to adjust the hide. She offered very little in the way of encouragement.

When I was nearly finished, I asked, "Do you think this is a decent job?"

Agnes looked doubtful. "The hide must be tighter," she said. Her eyes brightened. "I have something for you in the cabin."

I watched as Agnes went toward her house, disappeared through the doorway. In a few moments she was back. I felt a certain stillness in the air. She was holding several feathers.

"Here are some eagle feathers for you to put on this shield." She handed me three feathers.

"Eagle feathers! Thank you, Agnes."

I knew that eagle feathers were very important in her world, and each time I obtained one it was an important occasion. I examined the feathers and I was shocked.

"Agnes, these aren't eagle feathers!"

"Yes, they are."

"No, Agnes. I know eagle feathers when I see them and these aren't eagle feathers."

"What kind of feathers are they?"

I was embarrassed. "I think they're wild turkey feathers."

"I see you have no respect for turkey feathers."

"Well, they're not eagle feathers."

"I said they were eagle feathers," Agnes insisted.

"Agnes, forgive me, but turkey feathers can't be eagle feathers."

"They can and they are."

"Agnes, you have great power and you can sometimes make me think black is white, but you can't change reality. I know these are turkey feathers."

"You know nothing."

I was getting annoyed. Agnes had a very proud nature, but I couldn't imagine why she was trying to palm off turkey feathers on me. That was bad enough; but then to compound matters and insist they were eagle feathers seemed to me to be taking advantage of me. I became surly, grabbed the shield, and began working the lacing on the inside.

Agnes laughed at me. I looked up and assumed a posture of rightful indignation. I was beginning to feel very hurt. Agnes laughed again and stared at me as though I were the most ridiculous person she had ever seen. I sat motionless, but I was wilted by the prankishness in her eyes.

"No wonder we never got along," she said.

"Who?" I asked.

"My people and your people."

"Why do you say that?"

"They were all the time getting peeved at each other and much hatred grew between us. It was unavoidable, because my people had great pride and humor. Yours had the jitters and wanted to shoot those who were laughing at them. Yet I still find you white people very amusing. I have to laugh at you."

"What's so funny, Agnes?"

"You never let yourself go. Every word to you is a completeness or else a long way off. You like to bludgeon the meaning of something to fit your own stupidity."

"Are you talking about the turkey feathers?"

"Yes. You see, the turkey is known as 'south eagle.' You are making a south shield, so what better power to put on it? We call the turkey a 'buffalo eagle' or 'giveaway eagle.' We have such dissimilar languages. No wonder my people and yours were always at each other's throats. But it would serve you well to quit being so brittle."

"Is the turkey the buffalo eagle the same way the owl is called the night eagle?"

"Yes. When you make your night eagle shield, your heyoka shield, you will put deceiver feathers on it. Night eagle is clothed in deceiver feathers. We have deceived ourselves when we travel this world such as the curious way you believe a turkey feather cannot be an eagle feather. It's all in the meaning, not the name. The best thing for you to do now is to learn about deception and how to get out of it. You probably think turkey feathers are less valuable than eagle feathers. You are dead wrong. The noble turkey has given away so you can have those very feathers. Turkey feathers have medicine power, powers to teach us and powers to heal us. If you had ever hunted a wild turkey, you would know how greatly accomplished they are and what an honor it is to carry the feathers on your shield.

"The osprey is the eagle of the west—fishing eagle or dreaming eagle—the one we Indians call the beloved osprey. North eagle or day eagle is the one you call eagle. You see, to me they are all eagles, while to you who know so much about the winged ones—to you the giveaway eagle is the proper flesh to devour on holidays."

I felt my cheeks redden. Agnes shrugged her shoulders, turned around, and was gone before I could apologize.

I dreamed that night of painted shields and I heard drumming and fluting. Then I saw myself standing in the red-tinged light of a campfire. I began to dance to the beat of the drum. I was waiting for other women to join in the dancing, and I knew that many would soon be with me. As I danced, I felt a muscle cramp in my groin and in the small of my back. I realized that the fire was getting brighter and I was getting hotter. I woke up and unzipped my sleeping bag.

"Darn it," I said. "It's that time of the month."

I got up and took some tampons out of my backpack. Agnes was sitting at the table beading a small leather bag. She watched me curiously as I tore open the box.

"Woman, wait a moment."

My head jerked up to look at her in surprise. I wondered what this new confrontation was going to be about. I felt unaccountably dense.

"What are you going to do with your blood?"

"What?"

"What are you going to do with your womanliness, your blood?"

"I am going to use a tampon like I always do."

"Oh, that's good, my daughter, who chatters about symbols and the power of woman. Just use a tampon and throw your blood down some toilet with all the shit. That is a good symbol. Maybe we can put that on your shield. That should bring you a lot of power. That shows reverence for yourself and your sisters. I appreciate the way you civilized women treat the offerings of your body."

"Well, Agnes, what am I supposed to do? I can't just walk around bleeding. I know this is my power time, for four days anyway—but what can I do?" I was appalled by her tone and her use of words.

"That's a good idea. We will make you a hidden shield to go along with the hidden blood. We don't want anyone to know that you actually bleed. As long as it's out of sight, we can forget about it. Your warriors will like you better that way as long as they don't know."

"Agnes." I was bleeding and decided to just stand there. I didn't know what to do.

Agnes handed me a clean dish towel and, throwing some bread and cheese in a bag, she told me to follow her and wear a skirt. I quickly put on my clothes and I wore the dish towel. We headed down the trail to Dead Man's Creek. The morning was clear and crisp. I felt a slight breeze on my cheeks. When we reached the water's edge, Agnes walked more slowly. She reached down and placed her hands on one mossy patch after another. Finally, she found some moss that she seemed to like. There were poplar trees nearby and the moss was partially shaded.

"There." Agnes pointed to the moss with a big smile, showing her even white teeth.

"That's nice moss," I said, wondering why we were standing looking over the mossy banks of Dead Man's Creek.

"That's where you can sit for awhile while I talk to you about yourself. Moss is soft and gentle and will not hurt you. It is the oldest tampon. Sit there and give your blood to the Mother Earth with joy and know your power time. Your blood is sacred and speaks of your womanliness. Be proud of your time. It is not the 'curse,' as you white women call it." I took off my underpants, put the towel by my side, and sat down gingerly on the moss, crossing my legs. The cool moss felt soothing and good. It tickled me, and I couldn't help but giggle. Agnes sat across from me on her blanket and fixed us cheese and bread.

I ate hungrily. Agnes was looking at the passing water of the stream. She began to speak very quietly, "As we women are related to the water, it is good to be near moving water during your moon. We are born of the first words of the first mother. We are of the void and we carry the void. Our blood is her body. It is sacred. It is said she was born of the water and the earth, and that is why your blood shall return to the earth and your spirit to the waters of the sacred dream. Her power shall be honored over all the earth, and all men shall know her as the beginning. And now that you have transformed your body into the womb time, take care that your blood seed of our first mother is welcomed in a sacred way, for it is of her body. Her flesh has been burned that you may be given life. Her smoke will bring wisdom to your way. Smoke is a gift from the first mother's heart. Bless her memory, for she lives within you. When you eat, it is she who eats. When you smoke, it is she who takes your message to the faraway. When you bleed, it is she who bleeds. When you give your body to be divided in love, let all parts of you be in her name so that her love can be complete on this great earth.

"For so long the memory of her who gives us life has been hidden. We forget that our moon is our celebration time for her life within us. Women in their moon have set themselves aside because it is their power time, their time to look within and feed their inner strength. Women do not take part in certain ceremonies at this time because their power is so great that it completely disturbs the power and the power objects of any man. Some medicine men wear ermine in the sweat lodges to protect themselves at this time, but it does not work. They trick themselves. In the old way there were special lodges for women in their moon, and most women of the camp would bleed near the same time. That is because our bodies adapt to the harmony of our sisters. In those days we slept and rose with the sun. Our working hours were the same, and you could say that we bled together because of the light of Grandmother Sun—in those days she was Grandmother, not Grandfather. So much has been forgotten.

"What is this great Mother Earth dreaming as she turns slowly in her slumber? This dark night seems to never end, and she will awaken one morning and shrug her shoulders of sleep and wonder and become angry because the bones of her body are being torn apart cell by cell. And what of that dark night within each of us that we cannot learn, but to be broken like an arrow as her great back will be broken if we do not awaken with her. What does her great earth body want with us burdening her? When she bleeds and cleanses herself will she remember who we are or just what we are becoming?

"While you sit here, dream to the great mother. Your lap is her altar. Put your essence into your prayers, as we put our blood into her life and ask for balance and understanding in this lifetime. Give of your blood that she may hear you in her dreams and remember us when she wakes."

Agnes stood. "I am going to leave you alone with her." Agnes bent at the waist and placed both her hands on the earth. Then she took a tampon out of her pocket and handed it to me. I looked at her in surprise.

"There is no reason not to use the conveniences of the civilized world. We need to be able to use all things that help us live with more ease. But as we eat with the thought of the great giveaway, we must use any device with understanding, so that it gives away to the fullness of our lives and does not take away our dignity." She turned and cupped her hands to the wind. Making the sound of a whistling elk, she walked off up the creek and out of sight around the bend.

Overhead, the sun was beginning to possess the sky. I lay down on the moss with the rays warming my body. The summer birds played in the treetops, and I curled my naked toes into the bank of the stream. I lay there the rest of the afternoon thinking of myself as a woman, and realizing how many cultural cloaks I still needed to shed. I was always amazed at how little I really knew about myself. As I lay there on my back, I felt there was a real exchange of energy between my body and the earth. The insects were buzzing over the dark river mud, the light of the sun through the quaking green leaves encouraged the scent of femaleness and new plant growth. I felt a very real connection, as we were breathing the same air in exactly the same rhythm.

When I walked back to the cabin, it was late afternoon. I worked on the shield until after dark. Before I went to bed, Agnes told me that the physical shield was finished. "What remains," she said, "is the spirit."

During breakfast the next morning, I felt wonderful. I was unaccustomed to such a sense of physical and mental well-being. Perhaps it was an illusion, but I decided to enjoy it even so.

"Bring your shield," Agnes said, after the dishes were done. "I want you to drive somewhere. Hurry. We haven't much time." I am always pressed for time, and Agnes loves to mimic me in that way.

I got the shield and followed Agnes to my car. I put the shield in the back seat and got in. "Where to?" I asked.

Agnes pointed. "Follow the road that way and turn right."

We had driven a little over an hour when Agnes told me to park. "Follow me," Agnes said. "Bring your shield."

I walked behind her for at least another hour. Agnes guided me down a path rimmed with cottonwood trees and sage. The air was luxuriant. There seemed to be a cool wind blowing from the southeast. I could see the grey tops of low mountains in the distance. The path ended at a swiftly moving river. I wanted to stop and rest, but Agnes pushed on. In a moment we rounded a turn and came upon a waterfall. The water fell from a rock shelf high above us, and we were now in a sort of cup-shaped area. Where the water hit the pool at the bottom, there was a heavy mist.

"This is beautiful," I said.

"There are many helpers here," Agnes said, indicating the falls. "They have told me that here you will see your shield. Can you find your way back to the car?"

"You aren't going to leave me out here are you, Agnes?"

"You will have plenty of company," she said, indicating the plummeting water. "Already I hear them speaking to you."

"Will you wait for me at the car?"

"No. Do you remember your way back to the cabin?"

"I think I do."

"You should have paid better attention, Lynn. Place your shield there next to the edge of the water." Agnes went on to explain that I should listen to the water for advice, that the water wanted to share with me. She said that I should use my ears. She told me to gaze at the spot where the falling water met the pool until it blurred. "This is the region of the water beings, the knowers of all things born of water. It is the doorway to the lower world where the ancestors dwell. It is here that your guardians may come to you." She said that I should not consciously strive for any mental state, but to dream; the water's edge was a channel of great movement and flow, and no matter what I did, the water babies meant to share with me. "I hope you find your way home tonight," she finished.

I nodded that I understood. Agnes looked at me sternly.

"Are you sure you don't want a ride back?" I asked.

I could see that she had no intention of waiting for me. "Go and befriend the secrets," she said.

I watched her go back up the trail, and then took my shield to the place she had indicated. I decided to relax and sing a spirit song. The sun glared off the surface of the pool and caused my eyes to tear. I looked out over the shield in front of me to the foaming water. I had no idea what to expect.

I chanted softly and watched for a long time. The loud drone of the water seemed to contain indistinguishable voices. There was an uncomfortable pressure in my ears. For a few seconds, a sound would grow louder and louder. Just when I would think I couldn't stand it any longer, the sound would return to normal.

Soon time started playing tricks on me. My thoughts, which normally seemed to march in well-disciplined formation, began milling about aimlessly—and a few of them wandered off with no idea of where they were going. For some reason, it wasn't at all frightening. In fact, I felt it was a rather humorous mental situation. I was no longer in command of my troops. My army was in disarray. I had a sudden insight that the ruler of this motley group was located somewhere in my stomach. I felt it there as a kind of fear, and I realized that the key to controlling my mind was in being critical.

"Making shields is dumb," I managed to say aloud.

My thoughts didn't snap to attention and line up in a tight formation, but I had certainly piqued their interest. They all seemed to be looking at me expectantly. I knew then if I could question and criticize they would jump to and do exactly as I commanded. I was not reluctant to do this, but it just didn't seem important.

I had another great realization. Criticism wasn't the only key to bringing my thoughts into abeyance. Mystery would serve the same purpose.

"Why make shields?" I asked.

It was then that my thoughts became like amateur detectives. I could see them stalking around like Sherlock Holmes, examining the clues with a magnifying glass. Each of these detective-thoughts would offer me an answer.

I realized that my mind was a kind of storehouse of energy. It was ready to go off in any direction. The energy that is expended by the mind is like an infinite stream of water.

The water that fell from over the cliffside was illuminated by the sun and shimmered like a necklace of mirrors. I was suddenly caught up in the infinite variety of light patterns produced within the cascade. I wasn't seeing or hearing in the ordinary way—both events seemed to come from the same source. Relationships and correspondences were unclear. My mind was seeking to become one with this pulsation. My "I" was trying to let go of itself and merge into this higher harmony. I was trapped in the moment and there was absolutely no way to get out. Nor did I want to.

I knelt on a sandy finger of land, the shield in front of me as the water from the pool swirled off around me. The falls, no more than a hundred feet high, poured into a dark grotto.

I began to look at the boulders near the falls. Suddenly, amidst the various forms, a great rock woman appeared. Her flint-grey body was probably fifty feet high by ten feet wide at the base. The rock woman had long hair and a rather curious face, and wore a wide skirt.

Within her rock form were many other forms. She was gazing at a point in the water beyond my shield. When I focused my eyes on this area, the sound of the water from the falls thundered. It grew louder and louder. The water twinkled where the rock woman gazed. I had a vision of Agnes holding the waterfall in her hand. It went up and up in the form of light. In her other hand, she was holding a shield from which a spotted eagle feather hung.

I looked back at the waterfall. The water was made of light and Agnes was still holding it. It originated from her hands. I followed it as it zigzagged upward. The sky seemed to revolve, to turn clockwise above me. I became extremely dizzy. I looked back at the pool and Agnes was gone. The sound of the water grew even louder. I tried to find the woman in the rocks again. Out of the falls came many jewel-like birds with rainbow wings. They fluttered by me. They were marvelous. It was as if the very rainbow itself had taken life and borne the magnificent creatures. They were hypnotically beautiful. Then I saw the rock woman once more. Her eyes were again staring at a spot on the water just in front of my shield. As I looked at this spot, the water began to eddy. It seemed to be vibrating, and I felt myself falling backward. I adjusted my gaze and regained my balance. The eddy became larger and began to whirl. I couldn't look away. It held me, spun me, spun everything. I knew the mighty woman of stone had sent this whirlpool. It roared and swallowed and became unbearable. Then a large shield came up out of the whirlpool. It was perfectly real and it was in front of the waterfall. The design on the shield was a mysterious spiral. I had never seen one like it. The succession of images was overwhelming. There was so much light, sound, and beauty pouring into me that something in me snapped and I lost consciousness.

When I came to, it was dark. I wasn't scared. I was lying on my side on the ground. I got clumsily to my feet and waded out to get my shield, which was floating on the surface of the pool. The moonlight glittered off the water and the rocks. I knew this was a place of great converging energies, and Agnes had obviously put me there for this very purpose. I felt a kind of lightheaded giddiness and I knew I must go. I said good-bye to the falls, the rock woman, and the power place, offering tobacco. I carried the wet shield and walked back up the trail to my car.

When I returned to Agnes's cabin in the middle of the night, I was glowing with energy and excitement. I was relieved to see a light on in the cabin, and was eager to tell Agnes what had happened to me. I burst in the cabin door. Agnes laughed at the expression on my face and got up to pour some tea.

"Lynn, I see we are going to be up the rest of the night. Sit down and tell me before you burst."

I was in a mood of exultation and words just fell out of my mouth. I talked for a long time. When I had finished telling her everything, we had drunk three cups of tea. Finally I was silent, waiting for an explanation. The boards of the old cabin creaked. The wind seemed to be climbing over the walls.

"Medicine power is the power to bring harmony and balance into your life and into the life of others. When you begin to balance yourself in a medicine way, you begin to see magical glimpses because you are telling the beings of the earth that you believe in beauty. As a storyteller you must understand this. You are becoming a woman spinner. To learn medicine is to spin or to weave the concept of life into tangible forms. To lift beyond your ordinary vision and see the forces that give us life. This is why I am teaching you to understand things with all of your being, with all of your senses. Your sight, hearing, taste, smell—all that you are as woman. What happened to you today happened to all of you. That's why it was magical, and that is why you became intoxicated. You dreamed beyond imagination into the space reserved for shamans, for seers. That lonely world where madness and genius meet is familiar to a medicine person. You are destined to walk there in the great mysteries of this dimension. Never think that you found this path simply because you have worked hard and long and through many lifetimes. You are now and forever on the ultimate journey, the greatest adventure—following your way down the good red road.

"Your symbol today was the swirl. Some call it the whirling logs or the whirling from which all things are born. What you saw was the gateway to your innocence, a spiral, an opening to the knowledge of your womanhood. The rainbow birds told of the colors of the rainbow—one for each of the ever-widening circles of the spiral and the feather for the shield from Spotted Eagle. The stone woman of the falls blessed you and welcomes you to her world of river stones. Put one in your inner shield."

I hardly slept at all that night. Early the next morning, I finished painting the shield.

We had our morning tea and I set off for Ruby's cabin to get her approval of my shield. It was good to be walking. I had not been on that trail for a long time. The old familiar pond where I once met my sister dragonfly seemed a remote but welcome sight. It was almost noon when I reached the pool's edge. I sat on the rock by the water and ate some jerky, laying my shield down carefully so it wouldn't get smudged.

I badly needed to reflect over the last months of my life. Everything—the shield, Ruby, the acquisition of so much new knowledge—seemed miraculous. Manitoba, with her sky ever changing, her climate always refreshing—the great peace pulled me ever closer to Agnes and her teachings. I felt nourished by her. Was it possible for me to continue my life at this pace? So much was new. Some days I wept inside for the many tiny deaths I seemed to suffer. At other times I thought that time is simply measure. There is no death; there is only metamorphosis.

I walked at a hurried pace and then ran for awhile. The silence was deep. I ran for a long time. My chest heaved and my breathing began to get heavy. I had always thought that the reserve had eyes in every rock and bush. I slowed to a walk. I began to think Red Dog was lurking somewhere nearby, ready to kill me. I had to push the thought of him away, taking a deep breath of the clean air. I hadn't let myself think about him for a long time.

I saw Ruby's cabin below. I had walked and run practically the whole morning, and her cabin seemed further than I had remembered it. I stood for awhile, taking in the place and the great solitude. Smoke was curling up out of the chimney, but nothing else was moving. Everything was peaceful. I stood for a long time trying to become as quiet as the day, trying hard to center myself. When it felt right, I started down the path.

As I approached, I heard muffled sounds from within. The door burst open and Ben came out on Ruby's porch. He had a handkerchief tied around his head and he began sweeping with a long-handled broom. Then Drum came out with a piece of paper. He knelt down beside Ben, and Ben swept up dirt onto the paper.

Ruby came out. Her behavior was very menacing.

"Do a good job, boys," she said.

"Hello, Ruby," I called. Even though Agnes had told me about Ben and Drum apprenticing to Ruby, it was a shock to see them. I had always considered them my enemies.

When I spoke, Ben and Drum were startled. Neither of them had seen me. Drum, who was kneeling with the paper, threw up his arms, scattering the dust everywhere. It looked like Ben had jumped out of his shoes.

"It's her," Drum said.

"You blundering idiots!" Ruby shouted, grabbing the broom away from Ben. She started hitting Drum with the broom end and then she turned to Ben, yelling at him in Cree.

"We didn't mean to be scared," Drum apologized. "She creeped up on us. I'm not afraid of her." He went on again, speaking in Cree.

Drum's eyes betrayed him. Evidently, both he and Ben were terrified of me. That made me feel just fine.

Ruby threw the broom down on the porch. "Now, do it right," she said. "And I want you to do the windows too. Never mind her." She nodded at me. "I'll deal with Lynn."

"Yes, ma'am," they both said.

Ruby turned toward me. "I've taken these boys on as apprentices, as I'm sure you've heard. If they give you any trouble, bust 'em a good one."

Ruby turned and went back inside.

I ventured over and stood there leaning against the porch. Ben and Drum were intense in their effort to clean the spilled dirt.

"Hello," I said.

They were both determined not to look at me and gave only a muffled acknowledgment. They went right on working.

I noticed a big change in Red Dog's former apprentices. Not only was their hair combed and tied back with pieces of rawhide, but their clothes were clean and cared for. They looked like entirely different people. Even their posture had subtly altered. I remembered them as disheveled, sloppy, and sometimes hunched over. Now they stood erect—chests out and shoulders back. They looked very neat and clean and collected.

I said sincerely, "You're looking quite well these days."

I expected them to answer in monosyllables again, but I got another surprise. Ben and Drum both paused in what they were doing. They were very polite.

"You're looking well yourself, ma'am," Drum said.

"Yes, ma'am. So nice to see you," Ben added.

I couldn't believe their good manners. I remembered back to when I first encountered the pair. At that time I thought they were the two rudest people I had ever met. They had inspired both fear and levity on my part. I classified them as opponents and had the notion that they were the sort of people who were to be considered deadly. And they had indeed meant me serious harm.

Just then, Ruby poked her nose out of the door as if she wanted to hear what was being said. Ben and Drum jumped back to their duties and swept faster.

"Lynn, what are you waiting for? It's about time you came in and had some tea. And bring your shield."

It was the first time Ruby had ever actually invited me into her cabin for anything. It was as though I had broken through some invisible barrier, and I was pleased.

Ruby's cabin was similar on the inside to Agnes's cabin—with one difference. The place was turned upside down. Every drawer in the kitchen was pulled out. An odd collection of mismatched dishes and jars were sitting on the counter top near the sink. July was sitting on the floor surrounded by a great assortment of pots and pans. She was washing them carefully in an ancient wash tub. There was a strong smell of lye soap.

There were two beds, one large bed and one that was more of a cot. The mattresses were folded back on both. A stack of sheets and blankets rested on a bentwood chair.

"Lynn!" July said, greatly surprised. She got up and gave me a warm hug and then very quickly went back to work.

"We can talk another time," she said. "Right now. . . ." She motioned towards her dishes.

I stepped carefully over the stacks of papers, clothes, and kitchen items that were spread over the floor. I sat down at a newly painted wooden table and laid my shield down respectfully. Ruby sat across from me.

"Did you bring me any cigarettes?" she asked.

"No, I didn't, Ruby. Was I supposed to?"

"Yes. Next time you come, bring me a carton."

"I'd be glad to," I said.

Ruby turned to July and spoke in Cree and then in English for my benefit. "Make us some tea," she said.

July began to find some drinking utensils. She got some herb tea that sat in the sunlight in a glass jar in the window and poured two cups, straining it with a piece of cloth. She sat the cups on the table.

"I want to be alone with Lynn," Ruby said brusquely. "Go outside and work up the woodpile. Tell Ben and Drum not to come inside. Make them keep busy. Those two will slack off any chance they get."

July left the cabin, without a word or an upward glance, closing the door softly behind her. I heard chopping and then I heard wood being thrown about.

As if Ruby sensed my thoughts, she said, "I keep a tight lasso around here. I do it deliberately because they have no chief within them. Neither do you." She turned her face in profile as if she were looking out the window. Something about the way she did it totally unnerved me. It was almost like she was going to spring at me from the side at any moment, even though she was facing away. I sipped a little tea from my cup. It was very good, and I knew I could easily develop a craving for it. I gazed around the sun-filled cabin. Ruby didn't say anything, and I felt like she was baiting me. I kept my mouth shut. I kept crossing and uncrossing my legs and fidgeting in my chair. Still Ruby said nothing. I squirmed, feeling more and more uncomfortable. I was absorbed with the idea that Ruby was going to be the first to speak. But the more I waited, with her bolt upright and looking out the window, the more I felt almost silly. I had to catch my breath. Ruby showed no sign of caring or noticing my shield.

Finally, she reached out her hand very slowly and took hold of my arm. Just as slowly, she squeezed it very firmly.

"I'm waiting for you to be still," she said.

My reaction was to be even more unnerved. She shook her head very slightly and continued. "What do you now know of the south?"

"Agnes told me it is the position of trust and innocence."

She cut me off quickly. "I said what do *you* know of the south?" She still didn't turn from the window. I talked for a long time about all that I had been learning. I finished by saying, "The south is red." Ruby had been holding her palms over my shield all the time I had been speaking as if she were testing its power.

"Do you know why it's red?"

"No."

"So if you don't know why it's red, what good does it do you to know it is red?"

"I suppose none," I said.

"Does red remind you of anything?"

"Well, yes—blood."

"So if you thought about it, you'd know that red of the south might have something to do with blood?"

"Yes."

"And exactly what do you think it has to do with blood?"

"I don't know."

"To bleed is physical, isn't it? We women are physical, aren't we? And don't we bleed?"

"Every month," I said.

"That's what I want you to stay aware of," Ruby said. "Indians say a woman's vagina is in the south. You have put your blood into your shield. It is good, but you still need to be told some things again. The south has power, and when you bleed, you are in your moon, right? It is a power time. A man has a monthly cycle, too. That's his power time. If he's sensitive and aware, he knows when that time is. He doesn't give blood, and so his power time is never as strong as a woman's. But for man it's different. When he takes power, he flies; a woman goes into the earth. A woman who is in her moon will take the power of a medicine man easily. She can overpower him. Some medicine men, when in a ceremony with a woman who is in her moon, think they can take more power from her—but it never works.

"You have clawed and fought and made your first shield. Your second shield, your west shield, is also important. For now, you must identify with the south—make your alliance. You must live in the inward south at will and remember the feeling of the south and never forget how to return there. In ceremonies and when you need the knowledge of that direction, you have to remember how to get there inside of yourself. Some medicine men have four winds to help them. A medicine woman can take four mountains. That means that she might take four husbands, a north, a south, an east, and a west man. If a west ceremony is needed for someone, she will use her west man—his west energy to help her in that ceremony. For some it works very well.

"You become conscious of your sex—your vagina. That will get you to the south. The south shield is the mother or mothering shield. As you know, it is law, to protect the children, to feed and cherish them. To protect the children, you must stay aware of the child within. Now repeat everything to me so I know you understand."

I said everything that I remembered.

She ran her finger around the rim of her cup. She looked at me fixedly for a moment. There was a strangeness in her voice when she asked, "Is it still time for you to bleed?"

"Yes," I said.

"Good, that is when you attract the powers you need."

Ruby then took hold of my shield and said she would keep it for a few days. She sort of grunted her approval of it.

We talked for about another ten minutes and then I said, "You know, Ruby, I am feeling so incredibly good and balanced from this shield, I don't really think I need to make any more of them. I really am feeling great."

"Is that so?" Ruby said, slowly turning from the window. She stood up next to me and gently ran her hands from my head down my body to my feet.

"How does this make you feel?" she asked, as she very firmly applied pressure to the outside of my right knee. A shock of pain went through my knee, shooting up the outside of my right thigh and side and into my right ear. An explosion of sound raged momentarily through my head and I was suddenly airborne, throwing myself away from Ruby with all my might.

"Goddamn it, Ruby! That hurt horribly," I yelled.

"You told me you were balanced. If you were balanced, you wouldn't have hurt at all. I was testing you to see if you had more work to do. I believe so, don't you?"

"Okay," I said, sitting back down and rubbing my leg. I was badly frightened. Ruby told me to leave without saying anything to July, Ben, or Drum. I was disappointed because I wanted to talk to all of them. She said for me to walk directly back to Agnes's cabin without stopping or resting.

I was exhausted when I arrived back at Agnes's. It was dusk. The evening sun was sinking down over the plains. Agnes seemed more than unusually happy to see me. We had dinner and I was still tired and still a little shaken, but Agnes wanted to talk. She asked me what had transpired. I told her of my experience with Ruby.

"If Ruby kept the shield, that means that it is finished and we can continue on the west shield. Ruby is very strict, but she is good for you. There is nothing the matter with helpers, some helpers. There are plenty of dangers in working with Ruby. However, as you see, she won't put up with any hesitation or idiocy."

"What do you mean?" I asked.

"Ruby is a very tough teacher. She can walk through someone's mind before they know what hit them. It's easy for her to do, but not so easy for someone who gets into her web."

"I understand that alright. By the way, I saw Ben and Drum today. They behaved like two moles—they were scared and so funny. And I also felt the presence of Red Dog today—too near."

"That is why we are teaching you the shields." She bent forward and patted my hand. "Don't worry—there is reason for everything and the shields will protect you and teach you what you need to know."

I studied Agnes's face for a moment. Her dark eyes were concerned. She seemed so loving and beautiful all of a sudden that I wanted to cling to her.

"Lynn, you must keep your wolf medicine very strong. Not only physically, but also in the dream body. I want you to dream tonight of your medicine and then write your feelings in story form in your journal first thing in the morning. Then read it to me. Now, let's sleep."

I set my journal next to my sleeping bag and crawled into it, falling asleep almost instantly after turning my thoughts to dreaming. I had a beautiful medicine dream and wrote it in my journal at dawn. Then I woke Agnes and read it to her:

Black Wolf, her mind seeing a billion paths, trotted out from the pines and sniffed the clean-smelling air. The trees became quiet, watchful, and the plains grew silent. The silver face of the moon was rising. One trail glowed in front of she-wolf's eyes and became a path that snaked down into the darkest reaches of the valley. Staying off to one side she followed it.

An electric melody of echoes touched she-wolf's ears, and she stopped and strained in anticipation. The echoes had drifted over the pine needle floor, bouncing like sonar that had been breathed by the mountains. She-wolf backed, sensing the rush of invisible waves that prickled at every hair on her delicate legs. She lifted her paws high, as if stepping through a warm marsh. Then suddenly the tide had passed. She stopped this countermovement and sniffed again, now hearing the fleeing echoes as they churned through the chaparral. She knew now which medicine place had sung and her eyes sparkled with pleasure.

The moon rose higher and higher in the night sky as she progressed along the dry wash—play-trotting towards the glowing red eye where the two-legged dwelled. She moved in a wide circle when she came to a wall of dark force rising out of the earth. Then she bounded up the side of a ravine, making a sweep away from the willows that were praying.

Once she was on top of the rise, she turned and looked back, calculating the distance—measuring the dancing colors that moved in circles over the floor of the valley. Black Wolf did not have far to go now. Her howl of celebration broke from her throat as she-wolf felt her kinship with Grandmother Moon who showed her face and seemed to sing back a sullen music of her own. Her paws gripped the moist ground as she came down from the rise.

The purple and mauve grass waved and flowed from the quiet touch of the wind. She-wolf's choice was irrevocable now and she continued her unhurried pace. She became eager and began to move faster. Ahead of her, toward the river, the shapes of trees were blurred in the distance. There, she-wolf knew, among the deep rocks, the unseen teeth of mother earth, she would come face to face with her sister.

Black Wolf ran. She gloried in the feeling of muscles straining, and of the night wind against her fur. Her paws met and parted with the earth, creating a hypnotic, drum-like beat that caused the glowing path to pulse. She stopped looking and listening. The woods were now just ahead, close enough to hear the leaves whispering together, and to hear the river moving on its way. The dust she had raised caught up to her, creating the illusion of mist. She moved on. In the shadows of the forest, close to the ground, there was a flare of white-orange light. She-wolf caught the scent and knew she had come to the place where her sister waited. She entered a small clearing, and heart pounding slowed to a careful walk. She approached the luminous figure ahead, avoiding the pools of moonlight that were splashed here and there. She-wolf chose to emerge from the darkness into the illumination just in front of the blanket. On the blanket sat a two-legged—young, blonde, and female. She was smoking her pipe over a medicine shield, the smoke rising in a spiral to join the stars overhead. She-wolf knew she must take her honored place across from the pipe. She sniffed the aroma of the sacred tobacco, her nose quivering, and moved her front paws to the edge of the circle, becoming one with the light as she touched the blanket. Sitting, the two-legged was the same size as she-wolf. Slowly their glowing eyes met. Understanding came at once and for eternity their gaze stayed together in the kinship of recognition. They were as one.

When I was finished, I looked at Agnes. She said nothing; she just looked at me, smiling, and nodded with pleasure.

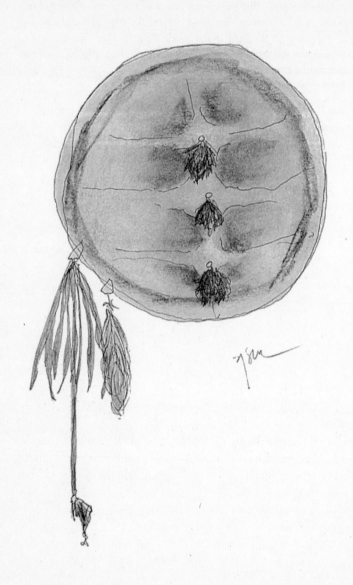

Dreaming-Bear Shield: West

Open the mirage that calls you . . .
     —PHILIP LAMANTIA, from
       Becoming Visible

Ruby Plenty Chiefs and July arrived at Agnes's cabin late in the evening. I liked July and wished we could spend more time together. Her long shiny black hair was beautiful, and her animated eyes seemed confident and friendly.

July was carrying some whitefish she had recently smoked. We all sat around Agnes's table as July unwrapped the newspaper. My mouth was watering in anticipation of the feast. I was feeling pangs of hunger, but Ruby reached over and pulled the newspaper back over the two fish. "Later," Ruby said. "First you must learn something."

I felt my hunger dissolving into frustration. It seemed to me as though Ruby was always snatching what I wanted out from under my nose. The formidable look on her face told me she would be unsympathetic to any protests.

"Soon it will be dark," Ruby continued, indicating that both July and I should listen. "Agnes and I are going to teach you and Lynn the medicines of your west shields. We are going to lead you underground into earth medicine. We're going to teach you about introspection. Introspection sits in the west. We are going to have a ceremony. Later we can feast on smoked fish."

I felt argumentative. "How can you show anyone about looking within since, by its very definition, it's inward and not outward?"

"Inward is outward," Ruby said with a force.

July and I looked blankly at each other.

"We are going to acquaint you with Shadow Woman," Agnes said.

"Do you mean the other side of ourselves?" July quickly asked.

"No," Ruby answered. "That would be heyoka awareness—understanding your true relationship with the Great Spirit. That is the Four Mirrors self and it is an eastway medicine. Like ants entering their kiva, we will go westway into the beneath, into the earth, into the places where the black mist is moving."

"To the place where prayersticks are driven," Agnes said. "Prayersticks are silent earth altars because they are masculine; they need female earth power for balance."

"We are going to the place of the great ripener," Ruby continued. "There are times when an apprentice will have big visions, and because of their bigness she will become unbalanced in her seeing—seeing everything as alive, every stone, every machine, every stick. But if your big vision is true, you begin to develop and see that some stones and, yes, even machines, are alive and some are dead. These dead ones have passed through the gateway in the West. It depends on the life within the object. You begin to see the sacredness in things, the energy, their colors, their luminous form—their shadow being."

As Ruby talked, it got darker and darker outside. She kept pouring herself more coffee, filling the cup until hot liquid touched her finger on the inside of the rim.

"At the westway beginning," Ruby said, "we chant the sacred chant. We dance with our intuition. It is gourd way. We are carriers of the Dreaming Shield."

Ruby rose and nodded to Agnes. Agnes got up and took a big bundle from under her bed and handed it to me.

"Here, this is what you will need. Don't open it now."

It felt like a sheath of animal skins. Agnes found a smaller bundle, which she slung over her shoulder. She gave another to July.

"Take your car keys. We have to drive about twenty-five miles—some of it on dirt roads."

We got in the car. Ruby and July sat in the back. As usual, we drove in silence. It was getting late into the evening. Thunder rumbled somewhere off in the distance.

"Turn right up ahead," Agnes said, breaking the long silence.

"It looks like another one of your cowpaths," I said smiling. I slowed and turned. The cowpath quickly dropped and we were driving down a ravine that looked like a crack in the earth. I was amazed as we pounded along the bumpy trail. The wedge deep into the earth was not visible from the main road.

"Very few of my people know of this place," She paused. "And none of your people." She turned toward me and smiled.

At the bottom of the ravine we turned abruptly, following along the edge of a marsh. We went perhaps a mile and Agnes ordered me to stop the car. We got out.

A great semicircle of cliff rose above us. I did a couple of deep knee bends, some running in place, and some deep breathing.

Ruby turned slowly, sniffing the air. From the bottom of the cliff looking up, I could see so many beautiful colors—shades of mauve, pink, red-orange, and grey going to tan. Its face was of sedimentary rocks, layered and worn and silent, like the bones of a Sumerian city eroded away and leaving only the faint indication that there may have been life there. The eons of rain and wind, and before that the erosion of water, had sculpted the perpendicular rock formations so that the surface appeared to have been rounded with infinite care by a pair of giant hands.

In a time of heavy rains, the runoff would rush in torrents over the edge and create a temporary waterfall—straight into the basin of jumbled boulders below. That ancient waterfall would have drowned us where we stood. I could imagine the shimmering fall of white water and hear its rush and howling power as it moved gigantic boulders and crushed them into pebbles—now a dark purple gash indicated the mighty flow that must often take place here.

Jack pine and tamarisk trees gnarled and twisted their way across the trail. I stopped to check the small, rough pine cones for nuts—they had already been ravaged by the squirrels. We walked quickly down into an arroyo sheltered from the sun by the awesome cliffs leaning over us. Clumps of sage dotted the dark earth and swept their branches in wisps across our path. Mouse trails and dear prints were the only tracks I could see. Small birds, perhaps white-throated swifts, darted into concealed crevices high above—every call, every movement echoed back to us and into the silence.

Agnes had called this place Heyoka Walls—the echoing mirror of every movement of life in the area. The cliffs taunted us as we crossed a marsh area and began our ascent up the face of the largest cliff. There were barely enough footholds chipped out of the grey rock, and we climbed carefully. Agnes led the way.

About halfway up she suddenly went around a cleft in the rock and disappeared. A few minutes later we climbed to the same place and turned: ahead of us was the dark mouth of a ceremonial cave. It was completely hidden from view unless one stumbled upon it.

It was sunset, and the purple shadows were growing larger. The wind had risen, blowing tiny particles of sand into my face. Crawling on all fours, I entered the mouth of the cave. Inside, I discovered I could stand. I wiped my eyes. The cave's interior, about twenty feet deep, was the size of a medium-sized room, and its walls were covered with petroglyphs and paintings. The scratchings on one side appeared to be ancient. The opposite side had been smeared with clay, and someone had painted designs over it with primary colors.

"This place is sometimes called 'The Place Where Crossed Arrows Are Drawn. This is a secret ceremonial cave. Never tell anyone where it is."

Agnes pointed to a large reversed-swastika design, like the whirling logs painted in red. "It is from the center, here, where the Great Spirit dwells." Then she pulled out several strands of her hair and placed them in a deep hole in the floor of the cave near the remnants of a fire. We all did the same.

"For the Grandparents," she said.

It was getting darker outside and the wind was making eerie

whistling noises. I looked to Agnes and Ruby for reassurance, but I could not read their expressions in the deepening evening shadows.

She took my bundle and handed it to me, then turned me to face the back of the cave.

For a moment it was very still.

"Come, all of you." Agnes took hold of Ruby's elbow. "We are going down into a hidden place of long ago. We have only a little further before we descend."

Agnes held up the torch she had lit. We all crept forward over the level floor toward a shelf of raw rock. Sitting on the shelf was a slab of flat, round granite. "It covers the doorway," Agnes said. "Move it carefully, for it protects the way."

July and I knelt down and, with a great effort, we managed to move the rock. I was now cold and clammy and a little frightened. Peering into the hole, I could see the first two rungs of a wooden pole ladder. It led down into total darkness. Agnes motioned for us to go ahead.

I had taken for granted that I was the only one frightened, but July grabbed my arm. She was shaking slightly. She leaned over and whispered to me, "Lynn, I'm afraid. We are going to be swallowed by the ghosts of our ancestors. They'll carry us off and we won't be able to return except in dreams. We're done for."

I took a deep breath. I didn't know what to say, but I tried to reassure her with a quick hug. But July's fear was contagious. I became desperately tense and then my own muscles began to twitch.

"First you, Lynn," Ruby said.

Stepping down the ladder was stepping into the unknown. My heart was leaping. I descended slowly into an undecipherable darkness like the underworld of myth. I clung to the ladder, full of anxiety. I looked up and saw July, who blotted out the torchlight as she began to climb down. It seemed a ravenous, almost tangible darkness, where all light was absorbed. There was no way of telling how far down I was, but it was much further than I had expected. The ladder must have been at least fifty feet long. When my feet at last touched bottom, I backed away from the ladder and waited for July and the others. I wondered what would happen to us if the ladder were to break. Would anyone ever find us? I looked around to see a shadowed cavern with a shelf at one end. It smelled of dry, dusty earth and there were partially obscured petroglyphs on the walls. I ran my fingers along one of the ancient ruts—a spiral curve with a snakelike figure at one end. I wanted to put a symbol on this wall and I wondered if, in another time, I might have left my mark here for other women, like myself, to be guided. Ruby followed July, and then Agnes came, carrying the torch.

Agnes indicated that we should all place our bundles at one end, opposite the shelf. She told us to try and read the symbols on the walls while she and Ruby prepared.

Shadows stirred now in the subterranean space. We were in a circular kivalike confine. Symbols were carved into the walls, which had been covered with a chalklike substance. There were representations of buffalo and hunters holding spears and knives; there were tipi and lodge signs and various other insignia, and many sacred symbols whose meaning eluded me. Ruby and Agnes were soon standing next to us. The torchlight bathed us all in gold, the color of wild honey. Shadows swayed over the walls like giant puff-adders.

Agnes stuck the torch into a crevice in the wall. Everyone appeared strange and distorted in the flickering light. The shadows seemed to mingle with the other parts of our bodies and then jump forward. My eyes were playing tricks on me. July's face would elongate like a Modigliani, and just as unexpectedly shrink back to normal. Ruby changed before me also. Her hips would jut out to the right, then pull back into themselves until she looked as thin as a rail. Agnes seemed to be growing out of the earth at her feet. It was a battle to hold everything in the proper frame of reference. I felt an enormous protection within these walls, as if I could fall back into the arms of the Great Mother.

"Remove your clothes and jewelry so that you may be painted," Agnes said. Her voice had a buffered quality to it in the compressed space. "You may bring nothing beyond this point."

"You must be painted too, July," Ruby said.

July and I removed our clothes and bracelets. Agnes painted me and Ruby painted July. "This place is called Dreaming Tree, and you are White Butterfly Maidens who have come here to learn."

Agnes painted me in various colors from the legs up. The design was unfamiliar, but there were bows on my arms and two moons near my breasts. "Here we can see with the eye of a snake. This painting is called 'Choosing the Path of the Altar.' I am painting you to set straight that which is crooked within you. I am painting you to protect you." She put a slash of color on my chin and two meticulous lines on my cheeks. I glanced at July, who was getting a similar treatment from Ruby. After Ruby and Agnes were finished, July and I were placed about five or six feet apart, facing each other. The paint on my body had a curious, prickly feeling, as though it were pulling on my skin. We were roughly squared off, with Ruby to July's left and Agnes to my left. Ruby began to chant, and then Agnes joined her. As the two old women sang, Agnes burnt sage, cedar, and a rope of sweet grass. The message of the song, I think, was to make our way sacred. For now there was still light, enough to see the looming figures of the other three women. I knew that soon the torch would be extinguished and there would be no more rippling firelight or undulating shadows. We would be covered in darkness.

They stopped singing.

Agnes knelt down and said, "We have blessed and banished anything unwanted here and balanced this sacred place. We are ready to begin the great teachings.

"We stand where two worlds come together, the spiritual and the physical. We are in the womb of our mother, the earth. All things are contained here." As Agnes spoke, she untied several bundles. Then she measured out various powders into pottery bowls. "We are in the passageway to the great dream. It is here when you descend that you are born, and it is here that when you ascend the cord is cut, and you are separated from your mother. But she will be reborn in you. You are her place of becoming, and we are in the lair of eternal return. Here you are going to learn to see what is hidden—to see with the eyes of a shamaness. Imagine that here you are a seed

within a sacred pod waiting to be fed and born with the secret codes
of all the ancestors within you."

I chanced a look at July. She appeared claustrophobic, her eyes
darting around. She wouldn't look at me. I felt slightly chilled, but
it was a chill from inside of me rather than from dampness. The
flickering torchlight was comforting. However, I was in such an
unfamiliar environment and circumstance that I was beginning to
feel unnerved. There was a heaviness on me and my muscles were
tightening.

Ruby told July to remain standing, and she led me to a knee-high
ledge a few feet behind us. She announced that it would take a
while for Agnes to make certain preparations that were needed. The
soft yellow torchlight seemed to pale from my new perspective.
Surprisingly, I was not cold. The earth was holding in our body
heat. I watched Agnes hunched over her bowls, mixing powders
together and praying in a low voice.

Ruby led July to a point about four feet in front of where I sat.
"Stand here in front of Lynn," she said.

Agnes stood up, holding one of the pottery bowls in her hand.
"Remain seated, Lynn," she said, coming nearer. Her shadow was
towering over us on the wall. "We are going to introduce you to
Shadow Woman. For you, Shadow Woman will come through July.
She will act as this principle. I have worked with Shadow Woman
for many years, and she has taught me something. If you look
around you, even here, you will realize that you don't see what you
think you see. The first thing is that we see backward." Agnes held
up her arms and crossed them. "Like this. The mind takes your
vision and readjusts it. When you talk to Shadow Woman you
realize that we have made other compensations as well. With
natural vision you can see energies, the lights coming off animals
and two-leggeds. But you have to perfect your vision to see these
things. Right now, if you learned to have true vision you would be
overwhelmed by what is really here for you to learn. It is too much
for the untrained mind. The two-leggeds have readjusted their minds
to accept very little. We have shielded ourselves against the sacred
vision. That is when a shield can be your destruction. It is a bad
thing when little children see the lights around plants, and parents

tell them they should stop lying about what they see. When you see shadows within shadows, you can enter the sacred trance at will and see and speak the truth."

Agnes held out the clay bowl in front of me. Words were difficult for her and she paused a moment. "Look at this. You should be filled with awe and wonder that this magical bowl can exist here as it has never existed before in the great dream. It is a tragedy for the world that they have taken away your eyes. They told you that the spirit of a thing is a lie, that your sacredness is outside of you. But there is one Great Spirit, and within him the many spirits are born."

Ruby extinguished the torch and all of a sudden we were swallowed in a deep darkness. "There are ways to bring spirits into the light and remember them," Agnes continued. "That is what we are going to do now. Look at Shadow Woman. Look straight in front of you."

There was a moment of complete silence, total darkness. Then all of a sudden an explosion of intense white light blinded me and lasted for perhaps ten seconds.

I heard Agnes say, "Lynn, hold your eyes open and look carefully at July."

July looked phantasmagoric. She was bathed in the most vivid light I had ever experienced. It was caused by the burning powders Agnes had thrown in the air in front of me. July stood out so clearly she seemed almost like a hologram. Then the flash of light was gone and was totally dark again, leaving only July's perfect luminous pink form standing there. I didn't know if it was her afterimage or what but the total effect was shocking.

"Hold the vision, Lynn," Agnes said again. "Hold."

By now the luminous image was not so much dissipating as sort of lifting off to the left in a series of reproductions like the frames in a sequence of motion picture film. I began to think that novel experience reminded me of a fireworks display I had seen once. As soon as this thought crossed my mind, the luminous form went away.

"Next time hold your concentration longer," Agnes said.

The light exploded again. It was as though July had suddenly been hit with a searchlight beam of immeasurable candle power. The powder spit in the air and went out. I saw the luminous form of July's afterimage once more. This time it seemed closer and even more vivid. I must have uttered a sound.

Agnes said, "Don't talk. Hold the image. You are seeing what mother earth sees. This is how she knows her children and knows when they are ill. Look at that area in her right side. There is less luminosity there. Why do you think that is? Now what do you see?"

"There is a pinkish form there. Now I can see inside of her. I can see her skeleton."

"Describe the pinkish form."

"Now, she looks like an old woman. She's withering and turning into a grandmother."

"Now hold your mind still," Agnes ordered. "Now tell us what's happening."

"Look at those feathers. She looks rather like a giant bird. Oh, she's starting to fly away. She must have eagle medicine—bird medicine. Look at that wing."

"This time," Agnes instructed, "look and see Shadow Woman as a goddess."

Again there was a flash and July was illuminated.

"Oh my, she's young again."

Again there was a flash. July was illuminated and then the opaque form was there. July's radiant face was that of a little girl. The vision I saw transformed from a little girl to perhaps what July would one day become—that of a woman wearing buckskin with long fringe. The beads on her belt had a kind of glassy glitter within the afterglow. I could make out some symbols. Her hair was white and hung shimmering to her waist. She was carrying the sacred pipe. Her light form was holding it out to me. Then she began to elongate and fade—her image trailed off and up to the right as my eyes struggled to hold her. I was so engaged in watching this ghostlike form that I started to list to the right and I lost my balance. I had no sense of up or down—only a floating, unearthly sensation. I grabbed out, trying to stabilize myself, holding the wall with one hand and the ledge with the other.

Though it was completely dark, Agnes and Ruby were quickly on both sides of me, propping me up. Agnes said that these new visions were too much for my untrained mind, and that it was time for me to act as Shadow Woman for July's benefit.

I took July's place and the process was repeated again. I was momentarily blinded as the powder exploded in front of me. I could see nothing but white light.

"July, what do you see?" asked Ruby.

"Oh, Lynn, I can see you. . . ." Her voice trailed off.

"Hold your attention better this time."

There was another brilliant flash. When it died, July said, "Look Agnes, she looks like she has blonde hair to her feet. Her feet are golden and that belt—oh!"

"What color am I?" I asked.

Again there was a blast of light.

"You are golden white, if that is possible, and you look like some goddess from the north, maybe Norway. You look about twenty. You have the most beautiful hair. Oh my God, you've just become old." July was almost yelling with excitement.

The light exploded into being again. This time when it died, Agnes spoke. "Lynn, you're standing there showing us in bright gold your Indian self. You have long black hair and are carrying a warrioress's shield with a great blue eagle on it. Look at the belt she wears around her waist, July. Those are symbols of the dreamers. You look about thirty-five now, and now you're getting very, very old."

I heard July gasp. Then Agnes and July clapped their hands like two children full of excitement.

"What do you see now?" I asked.

"For a moment you appeared as White Beaver Woman, bringer of the sacred pipe to the Cree people," Agnes said. "We have no more to teach you at present. Remember what you have seen both of you." A great silence and darkness enveloped us. I could see for a moment into the incredible vacuum left by the forces of creation. A shadow was thrown by life itself across the stillness of my consciousness. I had seen in those flickering frames a glimpse of the source of power.

After the teachings, we climbed up the ladder and closed the entrance.

We built a small fire from the bundle of sticks Agnes had brought with her. We all sat down on the cave floor above the subterranean cavern. We recounted all that we had seen while Agnes and Ruby listened to us.

"I can't believe it," I said. "How old are these instructions?" I asked.

"They are ancient," Ruby said. "No one knows for how long women have been instructing each other in this manner. Long ago the shamaness would go down into the earth mother and go out through her naval in a luminous form. Only spirit can doctor another spirit and heal it. This practice is for healing the heart and the spirit mind."

"Lynn," Agnes said, "originally these teachings were south teachings from the land of kivas. As we descend, we learn of ascent. As we go into the earth, we also go out in spirit. As the ladder goes down, the spirit ascends. And the slower your body goes, the faster your spirit travels."

"This is the key to luminosity, isn't it?" I asked.

"Yes," Agnes said. "This is training you to see the luminous form of all things."

"This is a mother cave, a place of power," Ruby said. "Here we are near the grandparents. In the beginning, the kiva teachings were women's teachings. The women left the kiva because they used their power for growing corn. If they went into the kiva, women could not bring down power from an opening in the sky, and they lost the growing medicine. In the old way, this going into a mother cave was like traveling into the womb. Women don't always have the need to learn of the womb, but they have power over the mother cave. Heyoka women have always had this power and we can come and go as we please."

Agnes interrupted. "Ruby, I think we have said enough. Lynn looks tired. She looks like she's seen a ghost."

Two days after the teachings in the mother cave, the weather changed. I had gotten up in the morning after listening to the rain off and on all night. Agnes was out somewhere when I awoke so I decided to drive over to Crowley and fill up my nearly empty gas tank. It was early, and I could see birds waking up with the sun. As I drove, I put my hand in the pocket of my jeans and felt the small stone that I had taken from the mother cave. It felt smooth and good as I rubbed it between my fingers. I was glad I had it with me, for it reminded me of my experiences. Agnes had said that the stone was a great responsibility, that I had chosen it well, but that it required a warrioress's resolution on my part. She told me that the stone could do much to benefit me if I would learn to use it properly.

I drove around for awhile on backroads, and arrived at the gas station just as it was opening. There was an old Dodge pickup truck on the other side of the pumps from me. Six Indian kids were in the back eating popsicles, sharing licks with a big, yellow hound dog. I gave the attendant, an old Metis man, twenty dollars and asked him to fill the tank while I went to use the restroom. As I walked, I was aware of great bulky shadows over me. The light glittered on the wet pavement, and the smell of rainwater and oily cement assaulted my nostrils. I looked up over the old white and red painted gas building at the clouds overhead. They looked like blowing clumps of lambswool with rivers of blue shining through them.

I flicked on the light in the restroom and saw a typical gas station latrine—one stall, used paper towels scattered on the damp floor, the acrid smell of urine. The cold water faucet was slowly dripping. I locked the door. After using the facilities, I washed my hands and started to leave. I reached to turn off the light and open the door. As I turned off the light, a kind of suspension occurred where suddenly I had little sense of movement or gravity. I was outside of time and space. The only reminder I had of my real body was a constant popping sensation in my ears. As I touched the whitewashed cement wall and flicked off the switch, the wall turned into adobe, to dirt like the interior of a kiva and there was no door, no bathroom, no visible way out. All of a sudden, the floor and my body were shaking. I felt as if I had straddled an albatross on a transdimensional flight. Then, just as suddenly, it became totally still.

As I felt my way along the adobe wall, pieces of it crumbling in between my fingers, I realized I was in a small, round enclosure. I panicked. My body wanted freedom and I became heavy with terror. I put my back to the wall and slid down to a kneeling position. It was then that I realized I was wearing buckskin leggings that pulled at my knees. I heard slow and deliberate footsteps overhead. I yelled for help, but the footsteps remained the same, their precise cadence becoming even more distinct.

Then the footsteps stopped and I heard a "whoosh," like the sound of air being pushed at a supersonic speed. A sudden shaft of light pierced the darkness. I could see through a round hole above me. Two Indian men with long black hair had pushed aside a stone cover and were in the process of lowering a large rattlesnake into my kiva. Instead of crying for help and being afraid, a calm came over me. I began to sing in a language unknown to me. Irrationally, I knew that I was undergoing an ancient initiation ritual. I tried to stay calm and understand what was happening to me, but my mind fought me, terrified as the stone was slid back into place. I knew there was a snake near me—I could hear its quiet hissing. I was afraid to blink my eyes, so I closed them and began to dream, forcing my mind into stillness. I knew I would die if I didn't stay with my center.

Suddenly, the silence was broken by a curse. "Hey lady, will you please come and move your car? I have another customer." He banged on the door. "Hey lady, are you okay? You've been in there for an hour."

I could hear pounding, and then keys were rattling in the door. Daylight filled the dank bathroom. My eyes hurt from the sudden light, as they focused on the two Indian men who were staring at me. I was crouched against the wall by the wash basin, sitting on the floor. Something snapped and I stood up, brushing myself off and stammering, "I'm sorry. I wasn't feeling very well. I'm coming out right now."

Hardly knowing what I was doing, I quickly looked around for the snake and felt the painted wall around the light switch. There was no trace of either the snake or the kivalike enclosure.

I got into my car and drove off without waiting for my change. In my rearview mirror, I could see the two men looking at each other and then shaking their heads in disbelief.

It took several days for me to assimilate what had happened in the gas station. When I asked Agnes about it, she said, "You slipped into another lifetime."

The mother cave experience had truly opened my vision to other realities.

For the next several days, I prepared my shield. Agnes, with her infinite wisdom, was always there to guide me when I needed her. I did not work in haste. With the shield across my knees, I finally finished plaiting the rawhide around the willow rim. I tested it, and it felt balanced and compact. Everything was done except for the design on the face. Agnes told me to bring it, and she took me back to the mother cave.

Standing in the torchlight near the entrance, Agnes whispered that I would have to descend into the cavern with my shield, place it in front of me, and sit once more with the shield and dream. With shield in hand, I descended the pole ladder. I began my vigil by doing as I was told. I heard Agnes's voice from above, "Lynn, I must close the stone. I will know when you receive your teaching. Only then will I remove it."

I felt a surge of panic as Agnes slowly pushed the slab of rock over the opening. With each scrape of rock against rock, the light was slowly extinguished. I had a moment of claustrophobia, and then I became a bit giddy. I wondered if the past-life experience would recur. In the total darkness, I could only hear my heart beating.

Hours passed as I sat in the womblike darkness. I took a deep breath, trying to release the tension from my back and neck. I observed my breathing. Then I started bringing energy up from the earth the way Agnes had taught me. She would say, "Lynn, listen and feel the earth breathing beneath you. Listen carefully to her, lay down on her, and one day you will become an earth prophetess. You will be able to see the weather before it comes, six months away. You will sense rain and thunder and disasters before they occur. She will talk to you. To learn this better, open the energy centers within your own body. See the red of the center at the base of your spine. Then move up to the orange in your lower belly, then to yellow in your solar plexus, and on up your body to the top of your head."

By the time I had visualized all the colors, I realized that the usual white noise in my head was distinctly changing in tone from one center to the next. I was playing a chromatic scale in my head. I was enormously excited to discover this. I kept pulling the energy up and down with the sounds that I heard, intent on maintaining the vivid colors.

Suddenly, as I blinked, I was aware of a glow, as if a single glowworm had fallen in front of me. It seemed to jump from side to side, and to be located somewhere in the center of my shield. As I watched, it left a small, phosphorescent trail in a concentric pattern. I was so startled by this vibrating point of light that I wondered if my senses weren't playing tricks on me. The longer I stared, the wider an area the light seemed to traverse. Also, it was slowly changing colors, first pink and then a vivid red. The next thing I knew, the light was opening out from the center in a most perplexing pattern that made me think of one of those games that kids play—trying to move a BB to the center of a complex maze. I knew I was that BB bouncing from one dead end to another. There seemed to be no way in or out of the problem that had formed before my eyes. This phenomenon seemed to take my consciousness and imprison it within its formidable walls. I was stymied in both time and space, light and shadow. Within that moment I became jailer and jailed; I was my own undoing in my inability to think my way through the labyrinth. My awareness was in a trap. I struggled to get out, to pull away, to lift my head. When I did so, I saw two large, clawed paws were standing at the top of the maze. They were a luminous red. Frightened, I looked up quickly. Before me, a huge, luminous grizzly bear was staring into my eyes.

"I am Grandmother Bear," the form communicated to me. "Come dance with me, my daughter. Come live with me in the faraway where there is no hunger or thirst."

I could see every detail of the bear's massive body. She looked playful as she ducked her head, but I wanted to run away.

"I am too afraid, Grandmother."

"I will hold your hand and lead you through fear. We will walk the sacred road together."

"As I am now walking the sacred road?"

"Yes, face your fears, my grandchild. That is the medicine road you seek. Remember your womanhood. Remember who you are."

"Great spirit bear, what is the labyrinth before me?"

The bear lifted her huge paw and, with unexpected force, she swiped away the northern and eastern portions of the luminous maze, leaving long claw prints in the sand.

I jumped back.

"This is who you are," the presence said. She indicated the ruined labyrinth.

I looked carefully.

"Find the north and east within yourself. Only with them can you complete your way."

I studied the ruined maze in the sand, trying desperately to memorize what was left as it faded away. I looked up to speak to Grandmother Bear, but she was gone.

I sat in silence, in this dark place, still remembering the sound of the bear's voice. I seemed to hear it deep within me. I had a feeling of expansion that momentarily leapfrogged beyond the facades and presumptions of power and self-examination into the timeless world of wonder. I must have dozed off then, because the next thing I remember was Agnes sliding back the stone. The torch she held threw down a mellow shaft of golden light. It hurt my eyes at first. When I looked down at my shield, I began to tremble. There were claw marks on the face of the hide. I touched them and tears came to my eyes. Bringing the shield with me, I slowly climbed up the ladder.

What a blessing it is to see, to come out of darkness into the light of day. Agnes told me not to speak yet of my vision, to hold it in my heart. I had so much energy that I needed to talk, so I told Agnes my thoughts on the subject of darkness as we were driving home. My experience had placed me in a very reflective mood.

"Both night and day are good," Agnes said. "Both speak a language. The language of the night is different from the language of the day. The language of the night is within you. Most two-leggeds have forgotten the language of night, but it would be good if they remembered, for a long night is coming before the break of dawn."

Once we got comfortable back at the cabin, I told Agnes of my experiences with the luminous bear. She asked me for an exact description of everything I had done from the moment she closed the opening. She nodded as I spoke, and smiled approvingly when I told her of the colors and sound. I went on for a long time, trying to remember every detail. The night passed before me again in vivid pictures. For once, I knew Agnes was truly happy with my efforts. She stared at me while she was thinking of something else, and then brusquely got up and went over to a dresser drawer. She pulled it open and pawed through the contents until she found a small bundle of red cloth in the back. She brought it to me, placing it in my left hand and covering it with her right. Holding my hand, she looked into my eyes for a long moment. Her gentle eyes were warm and tender, and their light was a river of love pouring deep and far, far back into the recesses of my heart. I was completely disarmed.

She said, "This is for your shield. Sew it on the left side and paint bear tracks leading north. It will always be hard for you to create something new in the winter. It is better for you to work in the other seasons of the year. Know this about yourself and rest in the winter months with your ally, the great mother grizzly. It will serve you well to learn to dream to her, for her medicine is powerful."

I took the red bundle and carefully unwrapped the material. Inside was a pouch of brown and grey fur, and inside that was a bear claw.

"Thank you, Agnes," I said with emotion. I knew how precious these things were to Agnes. "Where did you get it?"

"When I met the dreamers, that was their gift to me. Its medicine is full and it will bring you much power." I gave her a big hug.

We were both exhausted. I splashed water on my face and crawled into bed. I was asleep before I finished zipping up the sleeping bag. The next morning I was awake before dawn. I got up and dressed quietly, leaving Agnes asleep. I crept out with my shield, bear pouch, and paints. I decided not to return until my shield was finished. I walked about a mile to one of my favorite places under some poplar trees on top of a grassy hill. I worked carefully all day. This shield had the quality of pulling me inside myself. When I returned to the cabin, Agnes sensed my need for quiet. She nodded approval over my finished shield.

The next day I spent a few hours washing laundry and writing letters. Late in the day I wrapped my shield in a blanket and put it in the trunk of the car. Agnes and I drove over to Ruby's cabin. We arrived at twilight and went inside, with the shield and a package Agnes had brought for Ruby. We put our things by the door.

Ruby and July were just sitting down to eat, and Ben and Drum were busily scurrying around preparing things and serving dinner. A candle flickered a pleasant light on the table. A fruit jar of lovely wildflowers added color to the scene. There was even a blue-and-white checked table cloth. Ruby invited Agnes and me to sit down and eat with them, and we accepted gladly.

"Ben and Drum can eat later," she said. I heard Ben mumble something. July winked at me. Drum's disappointment was obvious. But it was evident that they didn't dare complain. With downcast eyes, the two men shuffled around serving venison steaks cooked to perfection and mashed potatoes.

"Ruby, this is really a feast," Agnes said, hungrily slicing into her meat. Ruby paid no attention and just sat there with a petulant look on her face, looking like a ninety-year-old child.

"My coffee is cold," Ruby said. Drum picked up her cup instantly, poured the steaming liquid back in the pot, and refilled the cup. "Sure took a long time for dinner to get ready," Ruby continued. "It would be nice if it would be ready when I wanted it." She picked at her food. "We don't have any decent forks," she continued to complain. "Ben, bring me a napkin. There's no salt on this stuff. They never season anything right."

Agnes and I looked at each other questioningly over our plates. I couldn't imagine what Ruby was up to now.

"But we put on exactly the amount of seasoning you told us," Ben and Drum both protested.

"Well, you didn't get it right," Ruby snapped.

"Actually, Ruby, I think this is quite good," said Agnes.

"I don't eat mashed potatoes," Ruby said, ignoring Agnes's statement. "They're bad for your teeth. Drum, you know I don't care for them."

Drum's mouth fell open. "But you've always loved mashed potatoes."

"Well, I don't care for them now." She took a tiny bite and wrinkled her nose. Her attention was suddenly on me. "Lynn, what are you fiddling with?"

"I'm getting my vitamins."

"Get Lynn a glass of water," she barked. Drum hastened to comply. "Those pills sound like dope to me."

"Well, they're not. They're organic vitamins. We've talked about my vitamins."

"Dope is what it is as far as I'm concerned." She shoved her plate over to July. "July, I don't want all this. You eat it."

Ben leaned over, obviously starving. "I'll eat it."

"Ben, it's just like you to try to trick me and get my food." Ruby jerked her plate back. "Well, don't think I'm going to stand for it." She began taking huge mouthfuls of food. She ate everything on her plate and told Ben to bring her any leftovers. "Bring those extra mashed potatoes, too," she demanded. She ate the leftovers in moments. "These two healthy young men would steal food right out from under an old woman's nose," Ruby complained, talking with her mouth full. "After all I've done for them."

Agnes picked up the package she had left by the door. "Here, Ruby, some berries for your cupboard." Agnes handed the package to Drum.

Ruby pushed away from the table, stood up and put her hands on her hips, and said in a very cranky voice, "Why did you bring berries for my cupboard? Are you saying I don't have anything in my cupboards?"

Agnes didn't pay any attention to Ruby. She sat back down. "I just thought you might like them, dear," she said. She looked up at the cabin ceiling shaking her head from side to side.

By now Drum had unwrapped the package and I caught sight of Ben and Drum drooling over the contents.

"Well, we might as well have those berries for dessert. Drum, you fix them for us and don't touch one of 'em."

Ben and Drum looked at each other and sighed in resignation.

When dessert was over, I asked Ruby to approve my shield.

"Can't it wait until morning? Every time you show up around here I never get to spend any time with Agnes. You can both sleep here tonight. You can have Ben and Drum's blankets. I hope they're clean. Ben and Drum can sleep in your car.

I looked at Agnes for support. She shook her head and shrugged her shoulders.

Agnes and I want to be alone to play checkers," Ruby said. "You young people skidaddle out of here after you clean up this mess."

"Checkers," I said in astonishment.

"Yes, checkers. Do you mind telling me what's wrong with checkers?"

"Nothing," I said. "If that's what you like."

A few minutes later, the dishes were done. We cleaned up the cabin spick and span and stood outside on the porch in the moonlight, staring at one another and wondering what to do. All of a sudden, from inside the cabin, our ears were assaulted by gales of laughter. July and I stared knowingly at each other and then started to giggle out loud. Ben and Drum looked at their feet and kicked some gravel off the old boards of the porch.

"Hey, guys," July said. "Let's go down by Dead Man's Creek and build a fire. It's obvious Ruby and Agnes don't want us around. We can go talk."

Everyone seemed agreed, and we went down the trail leading to Dead Man's Creek, gathering firewood on our way. When we reached the creek, we found a level area and built a small fire within a circle of rocks. The ground was damp and the air smelled of rotting weeds and leaves. The water licked over the rocks in the creek and had a soothing sound. Drum told us a joke and got us all relaxed and giggling.

I asked Ben and Drum what had happened to Red Dog. The happy mood changed to one of tension.

"I don't know if Ruby would mind if we talk about this," Drum said seriously. With his moustache hanging to the sides of his lips, he looked more like a Tibetan sherpa than a Cree. He trained his eyes on me and they gleamed in the golden firelight.

"I know that Red Dog was wounded and very sick in his heart. He said that you had been empowered by Agnes. He said that you alone would have never had the ability to steal from him. He was angry and ran us off. He said that he had to go and find another woman power. He told us never to come back, that we were unworthy of forbidden knowledge. He blamed us for losing the power basket, and he said that because of our carelessness he was going to have to find new weapons."

"I didn't steal the basket from Red Dog," I said. "I simply took something that belonged to the elders, the marriage basket, and returned it to the rightful keepers—the weavers and the dreamers."

"That's what we meant," Ben blurted. "Drum and I don't mean to offend you."

"That's okay," I said, smiling. "Just keep your facts straight."

I realized then that Ben and Drum would never trust me. Their eyes were bright with fear and they would always suspect some trick from me. To these two men, at least, I was a dangerous woman and one to be wary of. The thought filled me with a curious pride.

"Has anything interesting happened while I've been away?" I asked.

"Well, there was something funny," July said. "One day this guy came up here and begged Ruby to teach him." She laughed and Ben and Drum groaned. Evidently, they knew the story.

"The man said he wanted to be a sorcerer. Ruby didn't say

anything. She just listened. The man went on and on about the
things he had learned in books. 'Why do you come to me?' Ruby
asked. 'I'm a medicine woman, not a sorceress. You know it all
already.' 'I don't care what you are. I need experience,' the man
said. 'I really want to be your apprentice. I've really heard
extraordinary things about you.' 'I think you ought to go back to
wherever the hell you came from,' Ruby said. 'Nobody knows
anything around here. We're just a bunch of hick Indians and
rednecks. Someone has been feeding you a line of bullshit.'

"The man wouldn't take no for an answer and started reaching
into his pocket.

" 'How much money you got?' Ruby asked.

" 'Six hundred, but I can get more.'

" 'Give it to me,' Ruby said, and she put it in her shirt pocket.
'I'll teach you. Come on with me. Grab that shovel over there and
I'll show you some sorcery.'

"The man followed Ruby into the bush. They got to some flat
ground and Ruby told the man to smooth it over. The man crawled
around and threw away the stones and twigs and pulled out the dead
grass. 'Stand facing west,' Ruby said. The man did so. Ruby drew a
long rectangle at his feet with a stick. 'Say to the rectangle, 'This is
a magical rectangle. This is my grave and I am food for the worms.'
The man said it. 'Now walk around this rectangle and say it four
times in each direction.'

" 'Are you putting power into the rectangle?' the man asked. " 'I'm
putting you into the rectangle,' Ruby answered.

" 'Oh,' the man said. The man started getting a little scared by
this time. But he decided to continue. He did exactly what Ruby
told him to do.

" 'Now take the shovel and dig a hole about four feet deep here
inside these lines I've drawn.'

"The man started to dig. Ruby went over and smoked some
cigarettes and watched. The man wanted to talk and ask questions
but Ruby cut him off each time he tried. It took the man the better
part of the afternoon, but he finally got the hole the way Ruby
wanted it.

" 'Now lie down in it,' Ruby ordered.

"The man was very uncomfortable and he tried to protest, but Ruby insisted he get into the hole. When he did, Ruby said, 'Fold your hands over your chest and say good-bye to everything you value. It's good psychology,' she said. 'Make it like a prayer. Give it all you've got. You know how sorcery thrives on emotion.'

"The man started crying and saying good-bye to his sisters and his car and his university degrees.

" 'Good enough,' Ruby said. 'You must know from all your reading that earth has good emanations.'

" 'Of course,' the man said.

" 'So you will understand that while I bury you?'

" 'Well, I. . . .'

"By this time Ruby was shoveling the dirt over the man. the man jumped when dirt started filling his eyes, spitting and hissing. 'What are you doing?'

" 'I'm burying you,' Ruby said. 'This is your grave.'

" 'What are you talking about? You're crazy.'

" 'Oh damn,' Ruby said. 'I forgot part of the ritual. I forgot to smash you in the head with this shovel like the others.'

"The man lost his nerve, scrambled out of the hole, and went running off.

" 'Come back here,' Ruby yelled. 'Your grave is waiting. The worms are waiting.' "

We all rolled around on the ground, laughing so hard we were holding our sides by the time July had finished. When we had calmed down, Ben put some more wood on the dwindling embers, fanned it with his hand, and soon another nice blaze was going. We all stretched and got comfortable again.

"That reminds me of something that happened when I was with Agnes one time," I said. "We drove back from the store in Crowley and there was a big red Cadillac parked up on the hill. A man was sitting inside. He ran up to my car and asked Agnes if she was Agnes Whistling Elk. Agnes said she was. He said that he had been looking for her for months. 'What can I do for you?' Agnes asked. The man told Agnes his name and that he was a millionaire. He

said that he had a hunch that she could help him become a
financial avatar."

"What is a financial avatar?" Drum asked. Ben and July also
wanted to know.

"It's a person who realizes himself through money. Someone with
power like Ruby and Agnes, but finding it through money."

Ben and July and Drum all discussed this concept for awhile.
They were glad they were walking the medicine way, but all agreed
that money would be a hard path to self-realization.

"Go on," Drum urged. "What happened with this money guy?"

"Agnes told him that a strong hunch was a good motivation. She
said that it took courage to follow a hunch. She asked him what he
thought she could do for him. He said she could teach him and
wake up his other powers that would enable him to obtain even
more money. Agnes asked him what it was worth to him. He said
fifteen hundred dollars was a fair price considering that her needs
were simple. Agnes demanded more. They proceeded to haggle. I
swear it lasted for over an hour, back and forth. They finally agreed
on a price of three thousand dollars for Agnes's teachings. Agnes
told the man to give her the three thousand dollars. He counted it
out in hundred dollar bills into her hand. Then she asked him if he
had a match. He looked all through his car and he came back with
a wooden match he found in his glove box. She was sitting
cross-legged out on the hood of my car when he returned. Agnes
held the money in her left hand and lit it on fire. For a moment
the man was so dumbfounded he didn't move. Then he started to
cuss and he grabbed the burning money out of Agnes's hand and
tromped it out on the ground. He shoved the burnt bills in his
pocket and told Agnes she was completely crazy. He got in his car
and peeled out of there."

Ben groaned and everyone started laughing.

"There's more," I said. "I came up to Agnes and asked her why
she had burnt the man's money. She looked at me strangely. She
had a look of compassion on her face. 'I just showed that man the
answer he was looking for. Of course his trail is cut and he will not
reach the truth in his lifetime. He is too burdened by money to ever

understand its freedom. His hunch was right, but his faith was little. I hope he comes back, but I know he won't, and he will never find a guide.' "

I heard the cry of a loon at the edges of the trees amidst all our laughter. I was completely enjoying myself amidst these other apprentices. The scent of smoke lay in the air. I looked across the glow of the fire at Ben and Drum. The few pieces of green wood spit out an occasional explosion of sparks as the sap hit the flames.

"Is there anyone that Red Dog is afraid of?" I asked.

At the mention of Red Dog's name there was a distinct change in the demeanor of Ben and Drum. Their eyes shifted from side to side. There was none of the delight I had seen earlier during most of our conversation.

Ben started cracking his kunckles loudly and nervously and then he said, "Well, there was one man of power that really set Red Dog on his ear. He was not from Canada. I remember Red Dog telling us once about a ceremony down in Oklahoma where this shaman named David Carson did a most extraordinary thing. Carson came in and—"

Suddenly Drum shot sideways like a spring. He literally grabbed Ben's head with his left hand and covered his mouth with his right hand. Drum struggled to get away.

"You fool. You damned fool," Drum yelled in a hoarse voice.

Ben jerked away violently. It took a minute for him to get his wind.

"Are you crazy, Ben? He warned us never to dishonor him with that story. You won't be around long if you're that stupid. Red Dog will break us both apart."

Ben nodded his head saying, "You're right, Drum. You're right. He only told us that story to scare us." He spat on the ground, embarrassed.

I didn't know what to say, so I kept silent. Ben looked humiliated. July came to his rescue.

"David Carson sounds like a shaman to remember," she said, laughing. "Ruby has told me Carson is a heyoka, like herself. That's all I know. You guys are afraid of everyone. Enough stories. Why don't we chant for awhile?"

We started to sing a song to the great mother earth that Ruby had taught us years ago. As always, we got caught up in the rhythm and went on chanting for an hour or so until the fire had died down to a deep maroon glow.

Standing-Buffalo Shield: North

The Swampy Cree say stories live in the world and may choose to inhabit people, who then have the option of telling them back out into the world again.

This all can form a symbiotic relationship: If people nourish a story properly, it tells things about life.

The same is true with dreams and names. . . .

—HOWARD A. NORMAN, *The Wishing Bone Cycle*

Agnes and I went for a walk the next evening at sunset. We watched an eagle as it dipped and circled overhead. As we sat down on a grey outcropping of rock, the sun was lowering behind massive boulders, their silhouette etched in black against the rose colored sky. The wind was blowing from the southwest, carrying the scent of summer grasses, and the green breezes were balmy and warm. The movement of the dark shadows across the rocks was hypnotic, lulling me to sleep.

Suddenly, I was startled into alertness. There, standing alone in the crevice of the rocks, about three hundred yards away, was the figure of a man. He stood very still, a black cut-out against the sky. The outline of his beard glinted copper in the last of the light. I knew it was Red Dog.

"Agnes," I whispered. There was no answer.

I turned to get her attention. She was dozing. I held my breath and shook her gently awake.

"Over there. It's Red Dog," I whispered urgently. I motioned with my head and watched Agnes's reactions. Without turning her head, her eyes were alert. She frowned.

"Where?"

"Over there." I turned to indicate the direction, hearing a raven calling off to my left. Another raven answered from my right.

"He was there. I saw him."

Agnes patted my knee and said, "Are you sure you don't want him to be there?"

"Of course I don't."

"There are many who coax their fears, and the fears are sure to follow," Agnes said, and then laughed. "He's not over there. He's over there." She nodded off to her right and narrowed her eyes. When she said this, I saw a blur of light in the direction she motioned. I got a little dizzy. "No, he's over there," Agnes motioned. Again I saw a blur of light. I was sure I was going to faint. "No, he's behind us!" I jerked around involuntarily, frightened out of my skin. There was another blur of light and I fell to my left. Agnes grabbed me and steadied me.

"Agnes, what are you doing, trying to kill me?" My heart was racing. I thought she was mocking me, and I was going to pass out any second if she continued. She didn't. Instead, she rubbed the small of my back in a circular motion. It seemed to free some tension in my throat and chest.

"Quit coaxing, Lynn," Agnes said, patting my knee. "When you are hunting, one way to call your prey is to find a place in your mind that welcomes him. Your prey will become curious and come and you can have him. Your fears function in the same manner. It is the enemy luring you to your death. Quit coaxing and stay out of sight. Otherwise, you will draw your enemy and it might not go well for you."

"Are you saying my thinking caused me to see Red Dog?"

"Yes, you are asking power to bring him to you and you'd better stop, I warn you. You are bringing powerful forces to you that mean you no good."

"What can I do?" I asked, exasperated.

Agnes rubbed the small of my back once more and then she was silent. "Let's go," she said.

For the next two days, Agnes was silent. We had been so chummy recently that the sudden cold treatment hurt my feelings. Each time I tried to talk, Agnes put her hand over my mouth and shook her head. She didn't appear to be interested in teaching me anything. Then an amazing event took place.

As I was walking, near the cabin, I saw a woodpecker feather blowing on the ground. I picked it up but, while clutching it, I somehow dropped it. The feather was small, black and a sherbertlike raspberry color. I chased after it, grabbed it, picked it up, and then dropped it again. I was frustrated by my inability to hold on to the feather, and I grabbed unsuccessfully for it again.

Agnes burst out the cabin door and yelled at me. "Lynn, leave it! It is not meant for you."

"Nonsense," I yelled back at her, and chased after the blowing feather.

I never saw her move so fast. Before I knew what was happening, Agnes had me by the shoulders and was shaking me.

"I said leave it," she said.

"But why?"

She stopped shaking me. "That feather belongs to the windigo, the mountain spirit with a heart of ice. The feather belongs to him and he sent it to get you. I heard the feather telling you to come, and you were blindly following its instructions."

"Well, how am I supposed to know when a feather is saying something to me?"

"Lynn, I don't know what protects you. I don't have the slightest idea how you have avoided the many windigos advancing on you. There are many of them, and they are luring you to your death."

"You have mentioned the windigo stories before."

"I wish I could explain in my words. That feather has been taken by a spirit that gives it life and animates it. Almost any plant or animal or thing can be taken by a windigo. In this case, the mountain is a windigo. Do you see that mountain over there?"

"Yes."

"Never under any circumstance go there. There is no saving you if you do. For you, that mountain is a windigo, your death. The mountain sent the feather to fetch you and lead you to him. He has claimed you for his own, and for you he is death."

"Agnes, I've had the urge to go to that mountain often. The only reason I've never gone is that it's so far away."

"I assure you, you would never have returned."

I shivered in fright and promised never to go near the windigo mountain.

"How can I recognize a windigo, Agnes?"

"I see by your eyes that you are not taking me seriously, but I assure you I am speaking out of my concern for you. Some part of you does not believe me, but there is another part of you that knows the truth. Learn to dream when you are awake and then you will see what the Great Spirit sees. You will see the windigos that are reaching out to you. You will know when you are in danger. You won't have to die a foolish death. You can save yourself and you can save others. They say that the only way to kill a windigo is to melt his heart of ice. Don't be so easily tricked."

That night we sat on the porch. I rested with my back against the wall next to the door, and Agnes sat with her legs crossed and her hands on her knees. It had just turned dark and the moon shone through the clouds. An owl began to hoot.

The moonlight sculpted Agnes's high cheekbones.

"The old ones I used to know said keep it simple. When you make your bundle, don't make one of confusion."

"Do you mean innocence?" I asked.

"No, simplicity. It's quite different. I have seen you stumble over simplicity. You have learned great pyramids of knowledge. But if that learning is not exercised through experience, it cannot be realized. You are like someone with a new pickup truck and a new set of tools. Your truth is your tools. When you set out for the day's work, you leave your tools in the back of your pickup. Simple. You don't use them in the total circle of your life. Like most people, you don't experience with your whole self. That is the difference between knowledge and wisdom. Come inside. Let's have some tea."

We got up and entered the cabin. Agnes lit a lantern and I boiled some water. Agnes was sitting on her usual chair at the kitchen

table, her stocking feet curled around the rungs of the chair legs like
a young girl. I poured some hot tea from the teapot into both of our
cups and then sat down to her left.

"Look where you are sitting, Lynn. What does it tell you?"

I didn't know what to say. After a moment of thought, I decided
that if the table were round like a medicine wheel, Agnes was sitting
in the west, a place she had often told me was a woman's place of
power. I said, "I'm sitting in the north. Is that right?"

"Yes. Your body has taken its place in the north. You didn't
realize it, but you moved your chair clear around from its usual
position in the east. Your body learns wisdom sooner than your
mind.

"You usually sit across from me," she continued, "which implies
that you set yourself up for learning. Your body usually reads me as
a teacher sitting in the north, and you usually assume the position
of woman pupil sitting in trust and innocence in the south. But an
unusual thing has happened tonight." Agnes was quiet for a
moment. She picked up her cup and sipped her tea, but she was
watching me steadily. She started to chuckle softly, and I began to
squirm. Her eyes seemed to dance in the lantern light. I became
even more squeamish and was too confused to know what to say.
Agnes set down her tea and stood up, climbing up on her chair. She
threw back her head. She looked proud and strong, and very
agile.

"The whole consciousness of your race is obsessed with rumps."
She flung out her hip outrageously and turned around slowly on the
chair.

"Agnes, please be careful," I said, reacting to her rambunctious
behavior. She motioned for me to be silent.

"Every time you look through a magazine you see a dozen ads
with someone's rump in a pair of tight jeans. You people are
rump-obsessed, and there's a reason for that. Do you know what that
reason is?"

I was looking up at Agnes. "No, not really. Is it some kind of
obsession with sex?"

"Not entirely. What it really means is this." Agnes made a

sweeping gesture with her arm, indicating the table. "Doctors, teachers, and chiefs continually say, 'Look within yourself.'" She bent over from the waist as if she were looking for something in the center of the table. No matter where I moved, all I could see was Agnes's rump at eye level.

"What do you see?" she asked, patting herself on the behind.

I laughed out loud.

"That's right. When you look within, all you present to those following you is your fanny."

Agnes stood erect and, with one quick movement, stepped to the middle of the table.

"This is what you need to do, Lynn." She turned to face me. I stared back into her cunning eyes. "Stand within your circle. Turn to face those following you and look them square in the eye."

"You have quite a graphic way of making me see things, Agnes," I said. We were both grinning.

I hopped up on the chair in order to help Agnes down from the table. Instead of letting me help her, she jumped into the air. All that I saw in that moment were her pink and white socks. She landed softly on both feet, spun around quickly, and stood forward on one leg, as though in a martial arts stance. I, on the other hand, was off balance on the chair. Agnes strode forward and kept me from falling.

"Stay there," she said. "Let's see if you can keep your balance as we talk."

I felt a little ridiculous standing there on the chair, but when Agnes did it, it had seemed the most natural thing in the world.

"Standing on a chair will be good for you if you can do it." She let loose of my arm and took a few steps back. One chair leg wobbled, and it took me a moment to recapture my equilibrium. Agnes walked around behind me. "Don't move. Just listen," she said. "I'm going to knock you off. Be ready for me."

"Don't hurt me, Agnes."

"No, I won't touch you." She had lowered her voice an octave. "By moving your chair tonight into the north position, your body chose to stand within your sacred hoop and to stop that peripheral nonsense of looking within. Hold on to that view. Welcome to the circle."

Agnes's voice sounded like it was coming from the floor behind me and I turned to see where she was. I lost my balance and fell ass over teakettle from the chair. Agnes grabbed me in mid-air and somehow broke my fall. Then she helped me up.

"Come outside," she said. "I want to show you something about balance."

I followed her outdoors. We went about twenty yards from the cabin and stood in the moonlight.

"I want you to knock me down any way you can do it," she said.

"You're not serious, are you, Agnes?"

"Yes, I am. Knock me down."

"Do you mean push you down?"

"Try to knock me over. You can't do it."

"Sure I can."

"No way. Come on. I won't touch you."

Agnes kept prompting me to knock her down, but I was instinctively cautious. I didn't want to hurt her. I thought it would be an easy matter to unbalance and force her to the ground, especially if she wasn't going to resist.

"Okay, I'll give it a shot, Agnes. But don't blame me if I hurt you."

I felt my muscles tighten and I lunged at her. Instead of grabbing her, as I intended, I found myself on the ground. Somehow, Agnes had eluded me.

"Try again," she said. "Maybe you can do better next time."

I tried again. Agnes twisted her body ever so slightly to the left, and again I went down right in front of her. She laughed.

"You're not using enough force," she said. "Don't you want me to fall?"

"Oh, Agnes, I really do. I'm trying."

"Then get dangerous. Get mean and let me have it."

I charged at her with all my strength. Agnes swerved her body very slightly and all the air went out of me as I went down hard on the grass. I sat up wheezing.

"How can you do that to me? I can't get near you."

"It's my luminous form going out to meet your luminous form," she said, holding out her hand to help me to my feet. "The harder you try, the easier it is for me. My luminous form simply gives yours a tap and you are on the ground mostly by your own efforts. Don't look so bewildered." Agnes's eyes were glittering. "Enough of this stuff. Remember—you can use your energy efficiently if you are centered."

"Agnes," I said, trying to catch my breath, "take it easy on me, or you won't have an apprentice to work with."

"You think perhaps I am teaching you how powerless you are, but I'm not. You have the same advantages as I have. More, in fact, for I am old. I am helping you become aware of your potential. Let's sit on the porch for awhile."

We got comfortable on the cabin's porch steps. It felt very good to sit next to Agnes, bathing in her special aura. She rested her arm lightly around my shoulder.

"You are always faced with choices," she said. "You have the choice to nourish or you have the choice to destroy with your power. When you teach apprentices about power, it is very important to take them through their fears in the beginning, because evil and manipulation are caused by greed and envy, which are born of fear. To go through your own fears, you have to learn of yourself. It is hard to know of yourself without making an act of power or an act of beauty."

"What do you mean?"

"First of all, let me explain what I mean by power. That is a word whose meaning has been twisted in your world. When you say power, people become afraid. They think of the police and the tax collectors and someone having power over them. That is not what I mean by power. Power, in my way, is the understanding of the spirit of medicine energy that flows through all beings. A medicine person can translate that energy into healing and transformation for herself or others. Power is strength and the ability to see yourself through your own eyes and not through the eyes of another. It is being able to place a circle of power at your own feet and not take power from someone else's circle. True power is love.

"The problem is the same for both men and women, but for

women it is more difficult. How does a woman from your society arrive at wisdom? In reality, a woman is not powerless, and neither is a man. Because of lies, it is difficult for a woman to pick up the bow of authority in her own life. As a warrioress, Lynn, you must pick it up and learn how to use it. Many women look at the bow of authority as an object outside themselves and are afraid to pick it up. If you speak to a person who is standing in a powerless position and tell her to take her power, she becomes frightened because you are implying change. She must take a step into the mystery of the unknown to become powerful. If a person has power, as women do, and she doesn't use it, power will sit within her and have no place to focus. It is then that power becomes twisted and evil. It can turn against the person who has called it. If a person backs away from her power, she will develop back problems and all sorts of physical ailments. The greatest danger, if you have not walked with your fear and made it your ally, is that you will have no purpose and no direction and your power will become homeless and transient. It will destroy you."

"Do you know anyone that has happened to?"

"There are many," Anges said. "Let me tell you about an apprentice I once had. She was a good woman. She wanted to heal people and she spent her early life calling for power to come to her that she might use it in a worthy way. She studied all the wheels, all the counts, all the medicines. She was a dedicated apprentice, but she had one big problem. She had the strange idea that she had to control everything around her. She used her power to get a husband and children, and then she used her power to manipulate them. She moved away to Calgary, but her tracks led back to me from time to time.

"Envy and the need to control others is where witchcraft and sorcery are hatched. I believe you should never interfere with the free will of others unless they ask for help. This apprentice of mine began to use the medicine powers I had taught her to punish me. I cooperated with the energies she sent to control me. One day I surprised her. I stopped cooperating and began controlling her, much against my desire to do so."

"What happened?"

"I showed her unexpectedly her own fear. The mirror reflection was unbearable. She threw tantrums and tried in every way to continue to manipulate me. You must understand that her failure was her fear taking hold of her. She was unable to stand up to the demon of her own creation. Her fear had an enormous mouth and was devouring her life force. The woman was so eaten up by fear that she could only manipulate more. She could not face that devouring creature and let go of her.

"Because she could not face herself, she began to think I was the monster devouring her. She swore she was going to kill me by the very power I had taught her. She has tried many times, but so far unsuccessfully. She is still a prisoner of fear."

"Can't you do something for her?"

"No. I can't face her fear for her. She has to find her own courage. Anything I would do would only reinforce her great fear and prolong her pain."

"Does she have any power, Agnes?"

"Yes, she has great power and ability. She courted power, and power married her. But she can't move with it into an act of beauty because she is too afraid. She hasn't found her voice. I worry and think about her often. I send her love and good medicine every day."

We sat on the porch for a while, looking at the moon handing over the dark forms of trees. A cloud passed over, blotting out the moonlight. Agnes's voice was soothing and she said that it was time for sleep. As she hugged me to her, I felt secure and protected.

Early the next morning, we were rudely awakened by a pounding on the door. Agnes got up from the bed to her feet and shuffled to the door.

"Who is it?"

Ruby yelled from the other side. "It's Little Red Riding Hood. Who do you think it is?"

Agnes opened the door, stepped back and said, "Come in, Little Red Riding Hood."

Ruby strutted into the cabin carrying a big satchel. She exclaimed, "Why, Grandmother, what big eyes you have!"

Agnes growled like the big bad wolf and we all broke out laughing.

It was weird to see Ruby dressed up. She was flouncing around the cabin wearing a pillbox hat with a net pulled over the brim. She actually had on bright red lipstick. Her hair was done in a neat bun at the nape of her neck and a string of pearls hung over her flowered dress. In her stockings and black lace-up high heels she looked like she was playing dress-up. I even caught sight of a lace hanky tucked into her bosom.

"Boy, are you tarted up," I said.

Ruby ignored me. She faced Agnes, standing first on one foot and then the other. "Let's go," she said impatiently.

"Go where?" I stammered.

"We are going to see my cousin in the Pas. She's retired." Ruby threw herself onto a kitchen chair and sighed. She said sternly to Agnes, "Why aren't you ready?"

"Oh, I forgot. And I forgot to tell Lynn," Agnes said. She turned innocently to me. "We need a rest from all you kids. We need to spend some time with people our own age."

Agnes was pulling on her clothes.

"What about my shield?"

"What about it?" Agnes returned, rummaging around in a dresser drawer. She found a black purse, put it on top of the dresser, and banged the drawer shut.

"Well, what do I do next?"

"You make it. You don't need any more help from me."

"But how will I know if I'm doing it right?"

"By using your own judgment."

"But I need to have visions or dreams or something."

"So have 'em."

"But how?" I was working myself into a panic.

"You mean to tell me that after all this you don't know how to dream your own vision?"

Agnes had put on a blue and white polka dot dress, support hose, and brown low heels. Out of an old jewelry box painted green, she took a gold brooch, which she pinned to a white scarf around her neck.

"I thought you were going to help me? I was depending on you."

"I am going to help you. I'm getting out of here."

Following Agnes around the cabin, I whined, "Where do I go to have my north vision? Give me a hint."

Agnes and Ruby laughed, then Ruby said, "Lynn, why don't you go up to the North Pole? Isn't that where Santa Claus had his vision?"

"You two are trying to trick me. I don't believe you are going to leave."

"Oh yes, we are," they said in unison.

"Well, how are you going to get there?"

Agnes held out her hand.

I asked, "What is it you want?"

"I want the car keys. Give them to me."

"You don't even know how to drive, Agnes."

They both laughed uncontrollably. Still laughing, Ruby said in a loud voice, "Agnes can drive all right. I remember one time she ran three white guys off the road. Those guys thought we were a couple of crazy Indian women, so she proved it to them." There were tears in Ruby's eyes from laughter.

As Agnes went to and fro, quickly packing, I finally realized they might be serious about leaving. They started to go, carrying their battered old suitcases.

Agnes turned to me at the door and said, "Now don't forget to keep this place picked up and don't eat all the jerky."

I stammered, "When will you be back?"

"When it's right. Oh, by the way, give me twenty dollars for gas." She gave me a big smile.

We stared at each other for a moment. I was very upset, but I got my purse and rummaged through it and gave her the money.

"Agnes, tell me what I should do next on the shield. Which hide do you want me to use?"

"Does it really matter?" Agnes asked.

"Hell yes, it matters. It's crucial."

"Oh, Lynn, stop fussing," Ruby said. "You'll spoil my trip. A north shield won't help you much against Red Dog anyway."

Agnes and Ruby walked very quickly up the path to my car. Following along behind, I felt like screaming at them. They threw their old bags in the back seat and got in slamming the doors. I banged on the driver's window, where Agnes was sitting. She gave me a dirty look and opened it.

"Oh, what is it, Lynn?" she said, huffing.

"Aren't you going to leave me an address or telephone number or something? What if I want to get a hold of you?"

"Look, Lynn. We have touched and I think we will touch again. You can't write or call me from here anyway, so an address or number wouldn't do you any good. And besides, I'll have your car. Now which of these gears makes you go backwards? I can't stand these new-fangled transmissions."

"Agnes, you promised you could drive," I said in alarm. I had a fleeting vision of my car mangled around a tree and wondered what I would tell the insurance investigators. I imagined visiting Agnes and Ruby in some out-of-the-way hospital, with them looking like a couple of mummies in traction and me apologizing to everyone for giving them the keys to my technological marvel.

Suddenly, there was a grinding of gears and an explosion of dust as the car lurched backward, squealed to a halt, and then surged forward, fishtailing in the gravel. They were gone in a swirl of exhaust and flying debris. I stood there swallowing dust, facing the green and beautiful flats of Manitoba, and feeling totally abandoned and helpless.

I walked slowly back to the cabin. Confused and angry, I dug out a newly hewn willow sapling out from under Agnes's cluttered bed, found a large ball of rawhide, and put them on the table. I sat down and began bending the wood, trying to force a circle. My fingers slipped and the sapling shot out of my hands, hitting me in the chin and slapping loudly against the table.

"Those two old bats!" I swore. "Leaving me here to do this all by myself."

My hand and chin were stinging. I got up and kicked the chair. I poured a cup of sun tea to calm myself, sat down, and carefully began again.

Without Agnes there to guide me, I was apprehensive about each step in the process of assembling the shield. One moment I would be angry; the next moment I would laugh at the ludicrousness of my situation.

The idea that Agnes had left me did not bother me so much as the indefiniteness of her return. In my normal life in Los Angeles, I kept a calendar of scheduled meetings and luncheons. I had a relatively clear idea of what I would be doing from day to day and with whom I would be doing it. This gave me a sense of security, and I realized that I had made certain assumptions in my dealings with Agnes. Her unexpected departure had effectively jerked the rug out from under my feet. With Agnes, I could count on nothing. She had warned me: beware of certainty.

I imagined that she might not come back for a month, or maybe six months. There was no way I could stay in Canada for that long.

For a while, I worried about Agnes. What if she were to get into some kind of difficulty with the car? What if she needed my help? I finally decided that Agnes was a medicine woman who traveled all the time and had somehow managed to learn more and to get by better than anyone I had ever known. She would be able to handle herself in any given situation.

That left *me*. Here I was trying to build a power shield from a perspective of relative ignorance. I knew physically how to make a shield now; but I lacked the relevant teachings behind making it. I felt crippled. The longer I pondered my situation, the more I felt that Agnes had betrayed my apprenticeship. I began wondering if I could learn about the north shield from someone else. Perhaps some other medicine woman could empower me to overcome my limitations of knowledge and skill.

I realized how much I needed interaction with people. I

desperately needed to talk to someone. I began to talk out loud to myself.

I tried verbally to convince myself that I enjoyed the quiet and solitude. But, irrationally, I feared that every sound and dropping leaf was Red Dog. I was never frightened of him unless I was away from Agnes or Ruby, although I often thought that Ruby herself might be more scary than Red Dog.

I worked on the shield for the next several days. I reflected on the skills I had been taught, and I thought about Agnes and what she meant to me. Many sensations stirred within me as I began a new set of rituals now that Agnes was no longer around. Several times I addressed her, forgetting that she was gone. At the end of each day my heart became full, and I expected her to walk in any minute. During these hopeful moments, I felt as though the muses were dancing with me. I was at the beginning again, but I was seeing it for the first time.

I was not used to being alone and isolated. While working, I would lose track of time. The shield and Agnes merged in my thoughts; they were both a presence within me. I was overcome by the crowding images of my journey here to the north. Life as I knew it had been shrugged away.

Agnes had been gone over a week when I awoke in the middle of the night from a deep sleep to go to the bathroom. I lurched across the cabin in the dark, dimly aware of a clapping sound. Still half asleep, I thought I saw a dark shadow cross my vision as I opened the cabin door.

After relieving myself, I was completely awake. Cautiously, I came back inside and closed the door. My teeth were chattering like castanets from the frosty night air. I tried to calm myself by taking deep breaths. I became very alert, and my eyesight sharpened in the darkened cabin. Without warning, something brushed violently across the top of my head with a whooshing sound. I was too astonished to scream, and all I could think of was that Red Dog's spirit had somehow entered the room and was trying to get me. I dropped down on all fours, crawled forward, and crouched under the table. I pulled a chair in front of me for more protection, waiting. There was a crash and a spray of broken glass followed by the sound of wings beating the air. The thing sounded so enormous I was even more terrified, and pulled another chair to cage myself underneath the table.

Then there was another crash and splintering of glass hitting the floor. I must have pushed back so far that I was no longer under the table, for I felt the creature graze my shoulder and pull at my hair. By now I was screaming, not knowing what was inside the cabin or where it was coming from. I had just about lost all self-control, aware only of danger, when the moonlight coming in from the window was momentarily blotted out by the form of a huge raven battering against the glass trying to get out. There was blood on the window where the raven had continually beat its head again and again on the same spot. I was so relieved that this disturbance was not caused by Red Dog or one of his allies that I started to cry. I ran over and threw open the door and tried to shoo the raven outside. It wouldn't go. The raven even turned and flew to the door and then went right back to the window. At one point it knocked itself senseless, got up, and stood on the window ledge and pecked at the glass. It flew back across the room close to the ceiling, flew back to the ledge, stood there, turned as if making a decision, and flew out the door. I got right in bed and didn't move until I woke up at sunrise.

I was shocked to see Agnes standing at the foot of her bed, holding my unfinished shield in front of her. She was dressed as usual and holding an imaginary spear in her other hand, as though she were attacking me.

"Does your shield appear to have any power?" she asked.

"I don't know about my shield, but you certainly look ominous!"

"This place is such a wreck, I wanted to be ready for anything." Agnes laughed, propped the shield against the bed, and told me to get up.

"Agnes, as soon as I wake up I'll tell you what happened."

"I hope so. It must have been some party."

She lit the fire and made breakfast while I was dressing.

"Has any medicine happened to you?" she asked.

I told Agnes about my mental processes since she had left, all the things I had imagined. "Nothing's happened. I've just been scared out of my wits, that's all. Where have you been?"

"What were you frightened of?"

I told Agnes about the raven.

"Did you learn anything from this experience?"

"Well, I'm not going outside to pee anymore. I'm going to wait until morning."

I laughed, but Agnes was looking at me impassively. "The lesson to me is clear. That bird is you, time and time again, beating your head against an invisible barrier. No matter how long you persist on the wrong path you will never reach freedom. The bird had to stop and look around for another way out. Once she realized the way, with a very little effort she was free."

"How does that apply to me and my situation?"

"Maybe you're on the wrong horse. Maybe you belong in Turkey with those Sufis you were telling me about. Maybe you ought to be whirling around doing their dance of power."

Agnes's answer was so unexpected that I was momentarily stunned. Then I caught the twinkle in her eyes and we both laughed.

"I'm serious. How does it apply to me?"

"You think because I told you to do an act of power and do a giveaway, I told you to be a writer. But I did not tell you how to use your knowledge. You could have done many things, but you chose to put your tracks down on paper. I respect your act. However, now you think you are a writer. You are not. That is an expression of your invisible shield. You are a woman who is living her medicine, who did an act of writing, and you continue to define yourself by your acts.

"There are plateaus of learning in the life of every apprentice," she went on. She picked up the stick we used to stoke the fire and drew a zigzagged series of lines on the surface of the table. "When you reach the top of the mountain," she said, pointing with the stick, "you have to descend in order to climb the next mountain on your journey. Many times you will think your journey is over when you reach the top of the mountain. Do not be fooled. These are moments of great deception, like the bird flying against the window. You can sit on the mountain forever, saying, 'This is who I am. I am a writer. I am a teacher. I am a medicine woman.' Don't you see you are sitting on your own ego?" She erased the picture with her sleeve.

"What should I do when I think I've reached a pinnacle?"

"Let me tell you some rules about the different plateaus you will reach. When the shield carrier reaches the top of the mountain, she never seeks approval, because approval is based on doubt. A shield carrier has no expectations, is never awed by anything, has no beliefs, makes no judgments or comparisons. A shield carrier never competes. She considers herself in opposition with an opponent, not competition.

"These are the rules of the shield carrier. Remember them well. In your trust and innocence, never underestimate your enemy. In the west within your introspection, estimate and recognize any possible move your enemy might make. In the north, in your wisdom, know that an enemy can assume any potential. In illumination in the east, realize that a self army never exhausts itself in any manner. Standing in the center, you can see that a great warchief knows all the territories, inner and outer, in which armies exist. Remember that ignorance is your greatest enemy."

We talked for awhile longer, and then Agnes and I began cleaning up the wrecked cabin. When we had straightened up tolerably, Agnes told me to go and get several things from the trunk of my car. I was surprised at what I found: an owl wing, some old hides that might have been mule, pieces of broken mirror, a willow sapling, broken china that looked like something from the Ming dynasty, and some other things. I couldn't imagine constructing a shield from all that stuff, but I climbed down to Agnes's cabin carrying it all. Agnes refused to talk about the strange array of items, and told me to put them under her bed and forget about them. She told me to finish working on my shield.

Sometime after midday, Agnes asked me to follow her. We

walked over across the road and headed north down a shallow gulley and up on the other side. The wind was blowing softly. The ground felt relatively firm. There were patches of intense green blending into rich ochre, terra cota, and orange color of late in the season. It was getting to be early fall. Even now there was a hint of yellow in the quaking leaves of the trees. Here and there white wildflowers dotted the grassy plateau that reached endlessly to the hills on the horizon in front of us. Great shifting patterns of shadows moved across the flat land. They looked like giants born and reborn every other minute and then they died as the light changed. I looked up at the dapple of moving cloud formations as we walked on and on through the timeless daylight and the vast stillness.

Agnes stopped at the top of a grassy knoll. "Here," she said, motioning for me to sit down. She gestured at the sky where clouds were beginning to swarm.

"I have brought you here to show you the dance of the wind," Agnes said. She began chanting softly, her head bobbing forward slightly in the chant's meter. "Clouds," Agnes said, holding up her hand. "Flesh of the sky, become Lynn's teacher-helper." She continued chanting.

I watched as dark clouds rolled, lit amber and white by the sun. They began a slow spinning circle in the distance, patterning and repatterning. The endless succession of shapes and colors made me dizzy. Lightning split the sky, underneath the now-pancaked formation and there was a loud bark of thunder almost before the shard of light had disappeared.

Agnes said, "Ho!" to the lightning. "The great serpent twisting its tail and biting the ground. We sometimes say fire-that-falls-from-the-sky. Ho! It is my ally lashing her body of flaming light. It is good."

There was another tattoo of lightning and thunder below the distant clouds. Rain was falling from the clouds, but it was completely dry and clear for perhaps two thousand yards around us. The cloud which had been somewhat concentrated began to elongate. Lightning kept going off beneath it. The smell of late summer rain came toward us across the plains. I felt as if the clouds and the lightning and the rain were performing for us in a marvelous elemental play. The show was exhilarating. "Watch carefully now, Lynn. A magical being is about to show herself. She is the jeweled mist known as rainbow."

Right on schedule, a beautiful, high-arched rainbow made its appearance.

"Oh, it's beautiful, Agnes. Perfection."

"Yes, she crosses the world over and has brought us harmony.

"A rainbow is a great teacher. She has come as a helper. Her spirit presence sought you out, so catch her and learn from her before she vanishes."

"What do you mean?"

"She has come to teach you about thought."

"What should I do? How can she help me?"

"By remembering you are in the north. Ask yourself the question, 'How is she like my thoughts?' "

"How?"

"A rainbow appears to be a connecting link from one point to another point. The same is true of thought. She has no beginning and no ending. This also is true of thought. You can't catch hold of a rainbow; you can't catch hold of thought. She may be weak or strong, clear or unclear. The same is true of thought. She makes something where there is a semblance of nothing. So does thought. She is colored by the sun, the sky, the wind, as thought is colored by emotion. For some it is more difficult to go beyond thought than it is to go beyond this beautiful rainbow child."

The rainbow had already begun to dissolve slowly upward from its base. Then the colored line of light started to alter and break, and move slowly out of vision. I could no longer see the rain beneath the rainclouds, and the electrical activity had long since stopped. The clouds had changed, parting, they seemed to press apart and one formation floated to the left and the other to the right. The dark, heavy cloud mass had briskly evolved into a couple of billowing powder puffs.

The next day, I took my shield to Dead Man's Creek. Sitting on the trunk of an old withered tree, I worked on the stretched,

stiffened hide. I held it snuggled into my stomach. I was proud of
my work.

Crisp, golden leaves torn from the trees by the wind fell gently to
the mossy ground. As they blew by my feet, I realized that the
colder weather loomed ahead in the not-too-distant future. The
water in the creek rippled by, glistening on the rocks. The changing
season darkened my thoughts. Is life merely the process of dealing
with death?

Surely one day I will go to the land of spirits, I thought. Is life
pain and endless suffering, without reason or meaning? Is that what
makes pain unendurable? Does the concentrated act of creating a
shield make me waken to my higher self? Perhaps the work and the
symbols live within me and make my suffering understandable, and
therefore endurable. I looked at my reflection in the water, and
wondered whether the shield also showed me my reflection. I
thought about Agnes's words. "Say you are out of balance with the
great dream. That might be symbolized by a wounded bear on your
shield. The bear is a dreamer." So you take the medicine of the
wounded bear and symbolize it and put it on your shield. You
balance yourself with the dream."

I thought about the fantastic maze I had seen. Agnes said that a
maze was like a spider web, and that I had constructed a web of
words. I was going to have to unravel that web and find myself at
the center of the maze. Symbols, such as the wounded bear, were
the thread that would help me find the way. In the beginning,
Agnes had told me, was the spider, and in the beginning was the
Word.

My thoughts were pierced by a sudden fear that made me clutch
my shield. For an instant, I had the vague feeling I was being
watched. I looked around for confirmation. Above me, in a tree, a
squirrel hung downward like a teardrop and wriggled its tail. His
round, intelligent eyes appeared very interested in what I was doing.
Suddenly, the animal ran up the tree and out on a limb, jumped to
another tree, ran a few feet along another branch, and stopped. He
swiveled his head to look back at me, and then swished his tail back
and forth. Curiosity soon got the better of him. He came back,

jumping from limb to limb, returning to his previous spot, not more than fifteen feet away. The squirrel's frenetic grace reminded me of a ballet dancer or a trapeze artist.

I laughed at the squirrel's antics and proceeded with my work, ignoring him. The squirrel began making an angry chattering sound. Still, I paid him no mind. I quit working on my shield for awhile and watched the elusive blues and purples shifting on the surface of the creek water. Out of the corner of my eye, I noticed the squirrel had dropped to the ground and was standing at the base of the tree on his hind legs. He made such a loud scolding noise that I was forced to look at him. When I did so, he ran quickly back up the tree.

Again I decided to ignore him. He put up such a fuss at this affront, I decided he had a bruised ego. He was decidedly "squirrelly," I thought. Then I heard him approaching, still fussing and chattering. When I ventured a glance, he was not three feet away from me. It was almost as though this squirrel were trying to tell me something. He stood there defiantly, his red tail snapping and dancing back and forth, scolding me—or at least it seemed that way.

"Get lost," I said.

This really unnerved the old boy. He shot into the air like a spring. But instead of running back to the tree as I had expected, he leapt right on top of my shield and took a bite out of it. Then he ran, and so did I, screaming and throwing the shield off my lap and onto the ground.

I couldn't believe that darn squirrel. I was more afraid of him than he was of me. What was a squirrel, anyway, but some kind of overgrown rodent? I thought he might be rabid. I found a nice stick to use for defense and took out after him. I chased him around for awhile until he ran up the trunk of the tree and parked his red bulk on a limb directly above me. I began to search the ground for a rock or something when he threw a nut at me and struck me on the top of the head.

"Ouch!" I groaned.

I could see the headlines. "Lynn Andrews, known for her bizarre, quasi-Indian behavior, killed by a squirrel in a territorial dispute somewhere in the wilds of Manitoba. Reliable sources (the squirrel) indicate that Ms. Andrews was struck by an unknown missile while fashioning some unfamiliar Indian artifact."

"You win, you little twit!" I yelled.

As I went over to get my shield, Agnes showed up. She was doubled up with laughter.

"I've been watching you," she said. "That squirrel learned much wisdom from you. I hope you learned as much from him."

She put her arm around me and hugged me affectionately, still laughing. We walked along the bank of the creek for a ways. She told me to sit down with the shield between us. "I will explain the meaning of the squirrel's doings."

I relaxed as I looked across the shield into Agnes's dark eyes.

"Do you see some meaning in the squirrel's actions?" I finally asked.

"Yes. To the squirrel, you were a medicine sign. He came to learn from you. He faced his great fear and stole up to you to learn of your powers. He saw the energy of your shield and he wondered if he could make it reveal its power to him. The squirrel saw your shield better than you. The squirrel is very wise. Two-leggeds have learned from him over the centuries. He knows the turn of the season wheels and he collects food and prepares for winter. The squirrel knows many things about food that humans have yet to learn. They are familiar with tree spirits and tree magic. They know secret places of power, places that radiate with enough energy to drive the human crazy. They know of invisible places and will bring the love of one tree for another. The reason that the squirrel bit into your shield was to understand if you were making a food medicine to store away for the changing seasons. He thought of himself as a more dangerous adversary than you, but he was more frightened of your shield than of you. Even when you tried to chase him, he dodged you effortlessly. Even then, he didn't take to the tree trails. He gave away from his priceless possessions to your shield. Use that nut in your shield design somewhere, for it is good medicine from a friend who has given power to your shield. In return, I want you to go back and leave a pinch of tobacco for him at the base of his tree." Agnes stretched up her arms to the trees above. She chanted quietly, first in Cree and then in English:

> You are the squirrel spirit
> You walk the tree trails
> You are the gatherer squirrel
> You are jumper squirrel known in all worlds
> You are tree-memory, good-medicine squirrel
> You bring me light from the path shaded by leaves
> You walk the tree trails shining in the sun
> You are seer medicine-being
> You are shaman squirrel with your great warm coat
> Good-food squirrel, giveaway squirrel
> You are healing squirrel
> Teaching the tree alphabet
> Friend of woman-mystery squirrel.

Agnes's chanted words and the way she chanted them filled me with the most incredible strength and a feeling of glowing health. The creek seemed to stop flowing and become glassy, as if she were borrowing its energy. Agnes's image jumped out at me from across the shield, as if I had just put on 3-D glasses. I grabbed the shield to help me catch my balance. I thought it strange that Agnes also held the shield, not letting go. She started to pull at it ever so slightly. I took a firm hold and tried to resist. Still she turned it very slowly. When I stared again at Agnes, I experienced another optical illusion. This time, instead of her body snapping out at me, she seemed to draw back into the distance. I tried to convince myself that this wasn't happening. Although a similar phenomena had happened once before in my apprenticeship, I was becoming terrified. I wanted to take flight, but I was too panicked to move. I lost contact with where I was. I looked quickly down at my shield again to balance myself. To my horror, my hands were unknown to me. Something had happened to them. They were old, the fingers crooked and wrinkled, and the nails talon-like. I pulled up the sleeve on my left arm and it was also old and withered. I felt my face somewhat awkwardly, and my skin was crepey and dry. I pulled at my hair with my fingers and saw it was completely white.

"What's happening?" My voice came from deep within me and was nothing like the voice of my ordinary experience.

Agnes was another person. She leaned over the shield and was certainly not more than thirty years old. She continued to turn it until I was now holding the uppermost or north edge.

Now Agnes was even younger, a teen and then a child.

"Oh, Grandmother, please sing me your north song," the little girl said.

I didn't even know I knew a north song. But then I started to sing. My voice sounded like an ancient Indian woman was singing, vibrant, deep, and slightly hoarse.

> I came from the whirling lake
> The lake is my gateway
> I stand in the lake and know my death
> I am spirit woman
> I am word woman
> I write of my death in sacred time
> Sacred time is born of the lake.
>
> I am spirit woman
> I bring you light from the faraway
> A path lit by Grandmother Moon
> I am a gatherer of words
> My wolf trails shine from the moon
> The whirling lake brings forth my words
> I stand in the lake and know my death
> Shaman words return your spirit
> Lost spirit of the great earth round
> I return to the women of mystery
> The spirit words that have been lost.

"Oh, thank you, Grandmother. You have blessed me."

Agnes then began to advance closer in my vision and to age rapidly. I became conscious of my hands as she turned the shield so that I was again holding the south edge. They were back to normal.

I went blank and forgot to breathe. I fell face forward on the shield, gasping for air. I was wheezing for a moment, but when I caught my breath everything appeared normal.

Agnes was cocking her head to the side, staring at me and laughing. "Young lady, you'd better be careful. Old age is stalking you. I hope you like older men, Grandma."

"My god! How did all that happen to me?"

"It didn't happen to you. You see, we exchanged egos for a while. You certainly do need big medicine displays to bring you around to face yourself. I wouldn't bother dancing the ultimate inwardness if you didn't need it. The signs were right. It was time for you to be my teacher for a moment."

"What signs?"

"The squirrel and your reaction. I am not embarrassed to learn from an apprentice. I often turn people old and steal their youth," she said with a wink and a wry laugh. "How do you think I've lived to be this old woman you see before you?" She stood up and turned abruptly to leave, calling over her shoulder, "You'd better write down your north song before you forget it."

That night I asked Agnes what I was supposed to do about my north shield face. I wondered when I was going to seek a vision. Agnes clapped her hands together and then grabbed me by the head. She said that I was to put my experiences into the painting on the shield. She said that I had had too many visions for my own good.

The next day I felt very calm and relaxed. I began working on the shield face early. I painted a buffalo at the bottom or south of the shield. At the top I painted several stars representing the milky way galaxy and attached two beaded eagle feathers. When I showed it to Agnes, she indicated it was a very cosmic face. She said that it spoke of the giveaway to the great mind. She told me to take it over to Ruby's for her approval. Ruby was very pleased.

Fire-That-Falls-From-the-Sky Shield: East

Only let me speak my language
in your praise, silence of the valleys,
north side of the rivers,
third face averted,
emptiness!
Let me speak the mother tongue. . . .

—URSULA K. LeGUIN, from
Hard Words and Other Poems

I decided it was time for me to make my east shield. When Agnes left the cabin for a moment to get some wood, I leapt up and started to look under the bed for the materials she had told me were to be used in the construction of the next shield.

"Ah, ah, ah, keep your little hands out of the cookie jar."

I got up sheepishly. I turned to see Agnes silhouetted in the open doorway. She was shaking her finger at me.

"Very naughty," she scolded.

"Why can't I look?"

"You don't need to know," she snapped. "That's just the way it's done. Besides, you've already seen the shield makings once."

"I don't see how anyone can make a shield from that stuff. It looked like a bunch of junk."

"The east shield is no joke. It is the heyoka shield," she said walking over to the sink.

"It sounds mysterious. Will I be able to go to work soon?"

"Yes, perhaps, but first you must know your heyoka barrier. You will become the food of echoes. It is where the east shield is realized. Here you will find the great spirit wheel where sound copies itself. All things are held together by sound, and the slightest noise repeats itself many times. As the water's surface was the first mirror for the eyes, so the heyoka barrier is the first mirror for the ears. But it is more than that, for it helps the opening of your vision eye, the opening to forever. Just as four mirrors can teach you the simple construct of eternity, sound can shatter illusion around the sacred circle and take you there."

I had to squeeze Agnes's arm. "There you go again, Agnes, I can't follow you. What's the heyoka barrier?"

"It's a place, like a natural echo chamber, but it's much more than that. It will teach you about the other side of yourself. That's what heyoka is really all about."

Agnes was wearing a cocoa-colored Pendleton shirt, old and slick at the elbows. She pulled a mirror out of her pocket and handed it to me. It was round and looked as though it had been removed from a compact.

"I want you to use this mirror like the rear view mirror in an automobile. I want you to hold it out in front of you and watch very carefully what is happening to the rear. Be only vaguely conscious of what is in front. What is behind is important. You must watch very carefully. I want you to walk around just as you ordinarily would, but keep a sharp eye behind you."

"Agnes I can't imagine why you would want me to do anything so strange."

"It is a gathering of power and it will help you overcome the barrier. You may as well start right now."

Agnes took my shoulders and turned me to the east, then she moved my hand that held the mirror and placed it about a foot-and-a-half in front of me, at eye level.

"Describe what is behind you right now."

"Well, I see the logs of the cabin, the window, your herb bundles, and, if I hold it a little higher, I can see all the pots and dishes on the counter."

"Good. Now start to walk around with the mirror still held in front of you and tell me what you see. Hold most of your concentration on the reflection in the mirror. Now follow me outside."

Instead of the familiar sensation of going towards something, everything seemed to be moving away from me. My peripheral vision was obscured by this sudden change of perspective, and I couldn't rely on knowing what was just ahead.

"Lynn, move to your left. Move to your right. Good. Now I will give you a task. Go pick up that white rock and bring it to me."

As I walked toward the rock I had the sensation of standing still for a moment, because the reflection was always passing away from me. I handed her the rock.

"More attention on the mirror," she said.

She had me go pick up several other rocks and bring them to her. Because of the unusual spatial effect of the mirror, I would forget what I was doing and would have to stop and remember what task I was trying to perform. I did as she told me for a long while. Agnes constantly had me doing something specific like picking berries, getting water, or gathering kindling. This process went on for three days. Each night my dreams were very strange. The first night I dreamed of a girlfriend in Los Angeles who had an urgent communication for me. Her words seemed to float by me and I couldn't understand them. I would only catch a word here and there. I would wake up and then have the same dream again. I worked for two more days, holding the mirror up in front of me. My spatial perceptions became altered. It was very interesting and very confusing. At the end of the third day, Agnes said, "Enough. Walk around a little and get your bearings. Then tell me what you feel."

I handed Agnes the mirror. There was a curious sense of loss when I gave it to her. My eyes ached for a moment. I did some running in place and a few dozen jumping jacks, and sat down next to her on the steps in a state of agitation. Agnes was silent, waiting for me to speak.

"First of all, I realize that I see one thing when I look, but that a lot of other things that I'm not aware of are happening. It's like a difference in momentum from what I usually perceive. The world now seems more round. I have no idea what it means, but I'm fascinated by how things are moving away from me. Why are you having me do this, Agnes?"

"I have already told you that this is in preparation for your east shield. It is a chance to gather power. East is the only way to the center, to the core. When you were walking around and had the feeling that the world was standing still, this is the truth. It is a destruction of the world as you know it."

"That's for sure. It played havoc with my normal linear processes."

"Now the world will move back together differently. But it will only be an echo of what you knew before."

A crow cawed overhead and another answered from a thicket.

"The eyes have a closer kinship with the ears than you realize. Your eyes echo and this causes vision. Every object, every plant, animal, and human has a distinct sound. I have told you that Ruby is the Keeper-of-the-Face-of-the-Shields. Each shield has a unique face, as each human has a unique face. Each face makes a unique noise. Now I want you to go inside and lie on the bed and rest. See what your thoughts can tell you about the sound of faces. Then tell me what you discover when I return. While you do this, I will go to the tree and speak to her and make medicine for your east shield."

I nodded and went inside. I got comfortable on Agnes's bed and relaxed so deeply that I soon lost all track of time. I jumped when I opened my eyes and saw Agnes staring down at me.

I sat up and put my sweat socks back on. It was dark outside and Agnes had lit a candle. We sat down at the table.

"Tell me of faces," she said flatly.

"Well," I replied, "I suppose in love and politics and our daily affairs the human face forms an inordinate part of our consciousness. Take Helen of Troy. History says her face launched a thousand ships and burned the towers of Illium. Then there's art, of course. What one remembers in a Rembrandt painting like *The Last Supper* is the face of Christ." I wasn't sure Agnes understood my cultural references, but she nodded her head encouragingly. "I've never really stopped to think about how important faces are. I guess they form a large part of our reality."

"Yes, and what if one were to change faces?"

"How can you change your face?"

"Simple. By leaving yourself open or by putting on a mask. Mask-making is an ancient shaman art. We will speak much about this later, but I want you to think carefully and tell me if you understand. There are many kinds of masks. There are masks of people—warriors, dead shamans, masks that embody the spirit of animals and hunting objects; there are guardian spirit masks like the wolverine mask; and there are masks that stand up with the spirit of the sun or moon or the heart of a great hunter like the wolf. These masks can be magical and can bring powers in any endeavor, be it hunting, dancing for rain, fertile crops, or gifts within the mysteries of healing and dreaming. Think about your ability to alter your face—to become a creature alien to your usual sensibilities—to become a wolverine, for instance."

Agnes tapped my arm three times rather hard. "Quiet. Gaze at me very carefully and tell me what you see."

The candlelight flickered, chiseling deep shadows under her eyes. Her face became quite masculine, then the shadows underneath her eyes seemed to slant down along her nose. The nose became a snout and, instead of Agnes, I suddenly saw a bear sitting in her place.

"You're hypnotizing me again," I said.

"I am showing you a face," she said. "Who am I?"

"You are a bear."

"Oh, really?" In the blink of an eye, Agnes had become a lynx cat, her mouth open and dark like a starless night, snarling.

I jumped back. "It's facinating, but please stop. You're scaring me to death."

The lynx became a shadowed mass and was soon Agnes again.

"How do you do that, Agnes? Would someone else sitting here see what I just saw? It's so incredible."

"It depends on the person and how strongly I projected the image. That is what I am teaching you. I am showing you that what you imagine is true. Think about how you can change when you are in love. Love is a word for transformation. And there are many beings worthy of our love. It does not have to be a man you seek. When you say, 'I love you,' you are saying, 'I transform you.' But since you alone can transform no one, what you are really saying is, 'I transform myself and my vision.' I am always living in the lodge of love and I share it with you. Sound changes in certain states, such as when you are in love, or when you are learning from a teacher plant, such as peyote. I have told you that the lizard is a great ally. Did you know it can grow back its own tail? That is because it knows how to make its own sound. If you know how to make the sound of a thing—say, a rock—then the rock itself will soon follow. Great shamans have known these things, but it is a very dangerous knowledge and must be practiced with great care."

"Masks have the power to transform just like sound does."

"I understand what you say, Agnes, but aren't we all wearing masks in a way?"

"Yes. We are liars, deceivers—we have deceived ourselves. Perhaps I wear a mask as you know me. You think I'll do this or that, but you don't know if I'm wearing a mask or not. I have just shown you a bear and a cat. You think of a mask as being something other than your vision of me as a medicine woman. But how do you know I am a medicine woman? That may well be only what you see. You don't know. You can only guess, and that's because you don't know who is wearing a mask and who isn't.

"If you meet a person who is truly deceptive, there should be a mask somewhere he could put on that would be what he really is—and that's the heyoka mask."

I stared at Agnes. I had never thought about such things.

"Now go to bed and dream," she ordered. "You're tired."

Lying in my bedroll that night, I was wide awake. Visions of grotesque masks floated through my mind. I asked Agnes if she would tell me a story to help me get to sleep.

"There once was a warrior," she began. "The people called him Big Eye. One day he was walking and he fell into a pit full of serpents. He was there for several days and was bitten many times.

He nearly died, but at the point of death he went to the spirit house of snake where the great snake spoke to him.

" 'I will let you live, Big Eye, if you will do as I tell you,' the spirit snake said.

" 'I will,' Big Eye promised.

" ' Do not answer too quickly, lest you forget,' the spirit snake said.

" ' I promise never to forget you,' Big Eye said. 'I have seen what happens when one breaks a pledge to you.'

" 'And what is that?' the snake spirit asked.

" 'Then you become lightning in the sky, and I do not want to be bitten by you for breaking my promise.'

" 'You have spoken well, Grandson,' the spirit snake said. 'For it is true of my wrath.'

" 'What am I to do?' Big Eye wanted to know.

" 'You must promise to make four Inviting-in-the-Snake masks at the end of nine years.' "

" 'I will, Grandfather Snake,' Big Eye promised.

"So you see, the snake spirit let Big Eye live to become a great medicine man. Big Eye worked big medicine for the people.

"One day, at the end of the nine-year period, Big Eye began to work on the masks as instructed. A dance was to be given in Grandfather Snake's honor. Four male dancers put on the masks and danced.

"Big Eye said that he felt ill, and asked a friend to put him in his lodge and sew up the entrance. Inside, Big Eye began to shake and have convulsions. The snake spirit took him, and he slithered underneath the lodge hide. Outside, Big Eye coiled and made ready to join the women. The women saw him and welcomed him. One of the husbands, who was one of the masked dancers, took a stick and beat him, thinking the women were in danger. The snake tried to escape, so the women gathered and showed him a hiding place. He crawled inside a hole in a log, mangled and bleeding.

"When the husband upturned the log, Big Eye fell out, his snake spirit gone. He was returned to human form. He was unhurt and he went back to the dance as if nothing had happened."

The day dawned clear and cool. Agnes opened the windows and the door to let in the gentle breeze. Sun—or "houselight," as Agnes called it—streamed across the room. She waved her hand across the leaflike patterns on the table as if they were family pets.

"Here." Agnes handed me the small bead loom. "I have work to do today. Try and finish part of that belt you were weaving."

I took the unfinished work and went outside to sit on the porch. A doe raised her head from a patch of meadow not far away and stopped chewing for a moment. Grass hung down out of the corners of her mouth. She eyed me curiously and then went back to grazing.

I started thinking about masks and how subtle were the variations of defense. I deeply wanted to understand everything Agnes taught me. I felt the power of the earth growing inside me as I worked the threads in the loom. I was less afraid and more challenged these days, and I worked throughout the afternoon, barely noticing the passage of time.

Finally, I went over to where Agnes was sitting with her own beading. "Here." I held out the partially finished belt. Actually, I had made little progress.

"Hmmm," Agnes said, as she examined an inch or so of work, tugging at it here or there with her agile, brown fingers. "You're learning. It is good." She handed it back to me.

"What should I do now?" I asked, sitting down on the ground next to her. For some time she was absorbed in thought as she continued beading. Finally, she looked up and said, "You must become pregnant now."

"Pregnant?" I was astonished.

"Yes, you must embody certain things unborn before you can begin this shield. In stealing back the Marriage Basket from Red Dog, you learned to develop your womb so that it could become a proper receptacle for your prey. You concentrated your power in your womb so that you could accomplish the task. Now your womb is fertile for the planting of the next shield. The seeds you plant must be carried within you. You must be pregnant for the next meeting with your guardians. I'll tell you more. Why are you staring at me?"

"Agnes, how can you say pregnant? I can't be pregnant. . . ."

"Oh, you will be." Her stern face broke into a broad smile as she observed my distress.

"Oh, no," I protested.

"Oh, yes, there's more than one way to become pregnant in the eyes of the guardians. Don't worry, it is just a way to trick them. It's like a dance—their way of playing. No more babies for you or me." She was again laughing at me.

"Be attentive. We must make you appear to be pregnant . . . bind your belly with unborn things. I want you to find a certain wild bird's egg from a special nest and bring it here. Then we'll put it in a strip of wolf hide with some other sacred things along with forty-four seeds. All this will be wrapped around your belly with your beaded gourd and feathers hanging from it. It is very important that we do this egg thievery during the new moon tomorrow night. We had better go down now to the ravine and look for a nest."

"But, Agnes, it's getting dark already," I said nervously. "I can't climb around looking for eggs when it's pitch black outside."

"It's the only proper time. I will help you."

I followed Agnes into the cabin for a quick piece of bread and then we set out into the night, heading north down through the ravine following the creek. I tripped and stumbled along in the darkness. Agnes advised me to use the night vision she had worked so long with me to develop. Twice I fell, but Agnes shoved me ahead of her and soon we began to trot as my sight improved. Agnes growled at me and pushed us forward at a steady pace. I was startled again at how fast she moved. She was as agile as a young girl.

As we entered the narrow part of the ravine, I could see amazingly well. On either side loomed the craggy, eroded surfaces of the ravine walls, formed long ago when the creek was a raging torrent.

The porous granite was fairly easy to dig into. I knew of at least one fox burrow nearby. Agnes slowed, then halted abruptly.

Together we dropped to the ground to remain for a long time, silently watching the crags. Agnes had told me at the cabin that this was the home of what she called the elusive winter bird. In the late spring, the female bird burrows in the soft rock to lay her eggs high on the cliff face, safe from the four-leggeds. On dark nights, especially in the new moon, she would make short, swift flights to hunt the night worms and bugs that surfaced only in darkness.

Agnes had me observe certain cliffs jutting out to our right. I carefully studied every shadow and crevice. The granite there was higher and less accessible. The sheer walls seemed a likely site for a safe and quiet haven. I lay still, watching for what must have been at least an hour. Suddenly, a darting shadow swooped close to the ground and disappeared. Again it flashed by, only to fade into the cliff half-way to the top. I thought it was a large bat, but Agnes said it was the winter bird. I had found her hiding place within the first couple of hours—a sign, said Agnes, that I was going into my east power.

"I will leave you now. Find your way to the nest. I will be at the cabin." She handed me something that felt like it was made from furry animal skin. "Wear this mask when you are stalking the nest. It will help you as a stalker."

The mask was totally unfamiliar to me. I ran my fingers carefully over its face in the dark. Fur had been pulled away to give it design in places, and around the eyes and mouth. I pulled it on, and it fit over my head and face snugly and comfortably.

Agnes then left quickly. Without a sound, she disappeared into a stand of poplars. The most important thing Agnes had ever said to me about stalking was that the act of being a stalker was a great act of trickery, and never to let the prey know that you are enticing him or that you want him. For a second I saw myself crouched in the dark wilderness wearing a furry mask—was I really doing this? Then I centered my attention again. I wondered if I could climb up to that sharp overhang without the winter bird hearing me. What I wanted was for the winter bird to fly from her nest long enough for me to grab one egg and leave before she became aware of what I was doing. It was important for me not to disturb her.

I rubbed my hands and body with leaves so that the other eggs would not be contaminated with human scent and the mother bird would still accept them.

I began to feel a stiffness in my tensed muscles. I did not dare turn my head. My animal-skin mask was getting hot, and the leathery odor was fading. My cheeks felt like they were sunburned, and I had the curious sensation that the mask was molding to my features. I could not seem to make a clear definition in my mind as to where the mask left off and my face began. I felt increasingly warm. My eyesight suddenly changed. Various aspects of the expanse around me became more perceptible.

Lynn, the winter bird-stalker, I thought. I felt more and more like a four-legged who lived with her belly close to the ground. I crept forward a short distance. I kept feeling more and more like an animal. The sensation was voluptuous, each of my senses were intensified. My body was developing a mind of its own.

I was aware of the slightest sound—each gust of wind, each tiny noise, each snap, tap, and crunch. It was getting late, and I had no idea how long I had remained in my fixed position. But I knew when it was time to move. I searched out a long shadow extending from the base of the cliff and silently traversed it on all fours until I was directly under the nest. I was now not more than ten feet away, but I dared not move. I remained stationary, hardly breathing, waiting to see another darting bird shadow. Finally, it came—a sudden black shape moving in a narrow line off to my right. There seemed to be a dim light reflecting off the rim of the tiny cave nest. If I could step on a couple of large boulders, I could reach it in one leap.

Another winter bird suddenly swooped out of the nest, following the same path as the other. Stealthily, I drew forward and leapt to the top of the first boulder and then the next, hugging the cliff. I knew the mask was changing me in some manner, but it did not occur to me that my consciousness was also altering. A strange sound welled up in my throat as I felt for the nest. There were three eggs cushioned inside, and I took one of them.

I had a moment of extraordinary elation. For a second, I had acted on pure instinct, without rational thought. With incredible agility, I rose up and bounded into the shadows of the cliff. I was out of sight in seconds, running surefootedly through the poplar trees, carrying the egg in both hands. I was in a kind of delirium. An unfamiliar growling sound was coming from deep within me. I stopped a moment before entering the clearing, uncertain and watching. I put down the egg in the soft grass and tried to take off the mask. My face was numb. I panicked, the mask seemed to cling to my face. It had pulled snug under my chin and there seemed no way to get it off. It was as though I had become an animal from my shoulders up. I lay down on the ground on my side, curled around the egg to protect it. I kept pulling at the mask because I wanted to be done with the strange illusions it produced. But I found myself growling, and then it was all I could do not to devour the egg. The thought occurred to me that Agnes had given me a power mask for this very potentiality. My judgment had become confused, but I knew somehow that I was supposed to learn from the mask rather than fight it. I was imprisoned inside a wolflike consciousness. I knew that if I saw a wolf or wolverine, I would be able to talk with it in some ineffable manner. I wondered how many times I had been an animal in other lifetimes and wondered why most humans think that animals are somehow less conscious than people.

I lay on the ground like a small, furry creature, protecting my forbidden egg. I was growing weak, but my instincts for hunger and survival were growing stronger. I began to lick the egg gently. Suddenly, I was alert. I moved the egg down against my stomach, glancing around in every direction. I sensed danger, although I had heard nothing. I became aware of a set of remarkably bright eyes not far above me. Then an indefinite form lurched towards me out of the shadows. The mask was torn off of me and the egg was gone. Some instinctive rule of self protection had been violated. I became intensely disoriented and passed out.

When I woke up, I was lying on my back on the porch of the cabin. I tried to open my eyes, but my lids were heavy with what felt like axle grease. Agnes was sitting near me. She put her hand on the top of my head and her other hand on my solar plexus.

"Lay still for awhile," she said.

I had a bad headache just behind my eyes. I tried to sit up, but Agnes held me back.

"Relax," she ordered. "I want to talk to you."

She picked up the mask from her lap and held it out in front of me—just over my face. It was a wolverine.

"This is your death—one of them," she said, her voice angry. "All that's left of a lifetime. You were once the spirit of this being—a wolverine. And now I hold it in my hand in front of you—you who are watching through lofty human eyes. It could be a mask of stone or light or a mirror, but it is always a teacher through which truth emerges. You have worn so many masks. You have learned to blend in, to decoy. Few are aware that you're gathering knowledge every moment. You are the great impersonator.

"This wolverine mask is old and very powerful. She has the power to take you beyond impersonation and to bring you back to her living time. Tonight she came for you. You welcomed her. You were ready for the journey. I didn't know this mask was going to take you, but I saw many ominous signs. I hurried back to find you. I got there just in time. If you would have eaten that egg in the state I found you in, you would never have returned."

"The egg," I said. I tried to sit up.

"Here." Agnes held up the small tan egg. She handed it to me. "Careful," she said.

It was warm and I held it gently, unbelieving. I recalled the events of the night, but as if from a dream. Only my very tender face and the egg authenticated the struggle.

"That mask was so powerful. How could it transform me like that? You could have warned me."

"That would have robbed you. Once you have had the experience, that is the time to give advice. You were successful—a good sign. Come. No more talk. I think it is time to sleep."

It was late in the day when I got up and finally ate a little. I felt pressure in my ears and I didn't feel like talking. Agnes suggested that we go for a short walk.

When we went outside, I saw that she held an old gourd rattle.

Every so often, she would roll it over my head. It sounded different from the other rattles I had heard.

"Why does it sound so funny?"

"Because there are tiny fragments of jewels in it," Agnes said, shaking it and smiling. "The jewels speak to the crystal world if used in the right way. Precious stones hold power; semi-precious stones send power. Listen and hear her talk to you. She will take your discomfort away."

Agnes brought the rattle to my right ear and shook it. My ears felt like they were popping. It was also a soothing sound, and I began to feel lulled into a very relaxed state. It was a lovely sound.

"May I hold it?"

Agnes gave me the rattle. It was entirely beaded and peyote-stitched with old trade beads that were red, black, yellow, and white. An eagle plume was attached to the bulb end. It felt awfully good to be holding it. I rattled it continually as we walked. By the time we returned to the cabin, I was renewed. The pressure in my ears was completely gone.

"We are not going to eat now," she said, preparing tea. "We will drink some tea and rest. At sunset we will smoke the pipe. July and Ruby will be here. You will need all of us to help you flush your guardian. You will wear a special bundle as you face the heyoka barrier. It will contain the winter bird's egg, herbs, and the forty-four seeds belted around you. You will be taken to a place you have been before—we once shared the mother rattle ceremony there. It is a woman's place of initiation and power. You must be very strong, very tough. No coward will come back from the world of opposites alone. This is not a Sunday stroll. Facing the guardians is a very dangerous act. If your guardians discover your decoy, I can't be responsible for what happens. I will say one more thing. You must relax beyond the barrier. To be tight or rigid will fritter the experience away. You may shatter or break in half."

"Sounds like Humpty Dumpty," I said, trying for humor.

Agnes's look was stern and remote, and I became uneasy.

I rested for awhile until Agnes told me it was time to begin. She had me carry a stack of blankets to a small evergreen grove not far away. I smoothed a blanket out on the ground and Agnes sat in the west on top of it. She carefully laid out various items in front of her. Then she turned her attention to her pipe bag and took out the two pieces of her pipe. The wind began to stir and she wrapped a trade blanket around her shoulders. The black and grey colors faded into the hoary twilight.

The red stone of her pipe bowl rested in the palm of her left hand. She held it to her cheeks and forehead. Then she took the old twisted stem out of its wrapping of red cloth. Holding them both above her head and offering the pipe to her people, she fitted the stem into the carved bowl and her pipe was made. Out of the buckskin tobacco pouch she took out pungent dried leaves and crumbled them, putting them into her pipe with her prayers. Holding the bowl in her left hand and the stem in her right, she held it above her head and said more prayers to the sacred circle of her ancestors. Then she turned the pipe stem to Mother Earth that we may offer her our sacred smoke and walk the medicine path with White Beaver Woman, who brought the sacred pipe to the Cree people. She called in the powers of the four directions and placed tobacco and prayers in the bowl for all the living beings on the earth.

Agnes lit the pipe, her breath sucking the power of woman and flame through the tobacco until it flashed bright yellow and red in the dusk. I watched her face through the smoke twisting up from the body of the pipe. She turned the stem in a sunwise circle and handed it to me. I sucked the hot smoke through the wooden stem, drew it into my lungs, and it warmed my heart. I closed my eyes and dreamed for a moment of the powers above and below and cherished the breath of the sacred mother that I held in my lungs. It permeated my body and soul. I handed the pipe back to Agnes. She took it and held it up in celebration of the people, and separated her pipe.

She then smudged everything with smoke from a braid of sweet grass and began putting away her things.

I looked up to see Ruby and July standing behind her. I hadn't heard them come, and didn't know how long they'd been there. I started to say something to them, but Ruby motioned for me to be silent and to wait until Agnes was finished putting her pipe away. When she was done, Agnes reached over and patted my wrist.

We picked up everything. Ruby was carrying something large in a blanket, which she sat down on some flat ground about thirty yards away from where we had smoked the pipe. They turned me to face east, and Ruby put her hand on my stomach, pushing slightly.

"She is ready," she said to Agnes.

Agnes and Ruby stripped me of my clothes and handed them to July. "Take these off to the cabin," Agnes said to her.

July left. Agnes opened the blanket on the ground. Its contents had an alarming effect on me. My body tightened as I gazed down at a furry shape. I stepped back, not so much out of fear as out of surprise. Warmth flowed into my midsection.

"Protect her left," Agnes said.

Ruby stepped around and faced away from me on my left.

"What is that thing?" I asked.

"That is called Thunder Girdle," Agnes said. "It is your helper. Hold it and pray with it." She handed it to me.

July had come back from the cabin. I looked closer at the strange furry thing. It had the same dun color I associated with autumn. It was pear-shaped with a slightly concave area that fit perfectly under my breasts and over my stomach. Ruby and Agnes tied the bundle around me with strips of rawhide. I felt a little bit embarrassed. July was paying close attention to the process. A gust of wind blew her dark hair softly back around her face. When I looked at her, she smiled.

"I certainly feel different," I said.

"You are pregnant," Agnes said in a serious tone. "This is called the mothering way to trick the guardians. We have had good ceremonies and we know you are welcome. When you wore the mask you realized other lifetimes within you, and that was the proper sign."

"Why do I have to trick them? Is there no other way?"

"They like to be tricked, then they will honor you."

Ruby's eyes gleamed strangely. "Yes. To the luminous beings, you are with child. They see the luminous deceiver—the false life within you."

"Agnes, is that why you wanted the winter bird's egg and you went to so much trouble to find the forty-four seeds?"

"To fashion the luminous deceiver," Agnes said. "To make the guardians come to you and to pass you through the barrier."

"Don't you feel pregnant?" Ruby asked.

I thought about it for a moment. I felt very strange, vaguely sickened. If I had ever forgotten what it was like to be in the last stages of pregnancy, I quickly remembered. I felt like an oversensitive stuffed toad.

"Yes, I feel very pregnant. Will I be having twins?"

We all laughed. Ruby fastened a necklace around my neck. Attached to it were various pieces of broken shell, pottery shards tied with knotted string, old trade beads, and animal teeth, all twisted together.

I reached for the necklace to try to get a better look. Ruby caught my hand. "No," she said adamantly. "July, put the blanket around her."

July took the old blanket that had contained the Thunder Girdle and put it around my shoulders. If only the folks back in California could see me now, I thought. Agnes informed me that the blanket was a birthday blanket, that many infants had come into the world on the very blanket I was wrapped in.

Last of all, Agnes handed me a red pottery bowl with something she called a scratching stick protruding from the opening. She said that I might want the bowl and stick to collect something for my shield. I asked her what she meant, and she said the lesson was for me to figure out for myself.

We all started out for the same sacred place where we had done a rattle ceremony a long time ago. We went around past the right corner of the cabin and through a big crack in the black rocks that was impossible to see unless you approached it from exactly the right direction. We started down the narrow treacherous path that fell away to a sheer drop. I was careful with each step, and pressed my awkward and pregnant body against the smooth rock face to keep my balance. We passed through a shallow crease in the rocks and were standing on the steep-pitched rim of a deep chasm. One great wall at the east reared up proudly and massively from the floor of the ravine that looked nearly round. It was twenty or thirty feet across and looked almost like a prehistoric amphitheater. Instead of walking all the way into the area with me, Agnes, Ruby, and July took another trail and by the time I reached the bottom, they had reached the rimrock high above. They were standing at three of the cardinal points: July to the south, Agnes to the north, and Ruby to the west. I had been told to stand facing east near a small pile of stones. Facing east meant facing that sheer wall of stratified rock—purple, pink, grey, and black. I felt insignificant as I looked up its massive face at the reflection of the dying sun. I felt the west wind blow over me.

I sat the pottery bowl and scraping stick down at my feet, then I drew a sacred circle around me with tobacco. I imbued the line with power by saying prayers as Agnes had told me. It took me a long time to perform this opening ceremony, and I could feel subtle changes occurring in my body—an opening, a spreading apart, as in late pregnancy when your body prepares for birth. I began singing my birth song to the wall, and asked my guardians to make themselves known to me.

Agnes suddenly called out my name from the north.

"Hello, Lynn." The words reverberated, cracking the silence. The echoes repeated and then slowly faded away. Then July called from the south and Ruby from the west. Each voice affected me differently, touching different parts of my body.

All of a sudden, their voices called out my name in unison. "Hello, Lynn."

A torrent of clashing, tumbling sound assaulted my ears—"Hello hello Lynn Lynn." Over and over. I tried to draw inward to get underneath the deafening echoes, but my body was being shaken in every fiber. The echoes continued in a maddening sheet of sound. The fabric of my name echoed, wrapped around me like a cocoon, and I felt my body being shattered into tiny fragments that flew like sparks into space.

The noise continued, becoming deeper and louder. Fluttering like the hot, dry beating of the wings of a thousand bats next to my ears. I saw birdlike shadows going out from me as though they were bailing out of my body. I had no idea what these beings were, but I knew they were fleeing me. I thought perhaps I was dying and going back with the One, and they were losing their host.

"Why should you have the right to be born?" I heard a resonant voice say. "You have been that which is you. No one else can ever be that which you are and you have taken it away. Why are you being born when so many have died unjustly?"

The wall in front of me seemed to shift into two halves and split apart, revealing a serpentine light. It was as if a shell had been crushed, a shell that contained the sun. The light was impossible to look at. I had the terrifying realization that the light was reflected from within me, and what I saw was myself being torn from the great mystery of light into this world of darkness.

"Good-bye, Lynn. Good-bye, Lynn." It seemed to me as if the sound had merged behind me, into an entity that lived on its own, merging with my thoughts and pulling them apart. I spun around when I heard the voices. My first thought was that Agnes and Ruby had come down from the rimrock and were standing behind me outside the circle. What I saw were two pillars of grey luminosity.

"Who are you?" I asked. The tears of fear on my face felt cold in the wind.

"We are your teachers from the other side. You have been admitted here by the guardians. Instead of love, we teach hate. This is the truth. We are the left hand of power. We cannot deceive you. Instead of power we teach weakness. This is the truth. In our round, men are all powerful and men carry the void. We are medicine men who have given our power to medicine women. This is the truth. We are the charmers of pain and deception. There are no barriers here. Here we seek substance."

Had I thrown my body and senses away? I was terrified, and my terror was turning into an unbearable pain inside my stomach—long, tearing sensations like the pains of labor.

"Are you Agnes and Ruby?" I asked.

The luminous pillars of light began to dissolve. The forms that I thought might be Ruby and Agnes began to whirl and then were no more. Two young men stood there silently looking at me. They appeared aggressive, strong, lean, and wicked. They wore jeans, cowboy boots, and long-sleeved western shirts. They looked like younger male versions of my medicine women. I studied every pore of their dark faces, the muscles in their hands. I felt raped by this reality. How could this be happening?

Finally, I asked in a timid voice, "What are your powers?" I wasn't entirely sure if I had said it or thought it.

"We know all secrets, but we know nothing of the revealed. Ours are the heyoka powers that you have bid for beyond the barriers. We are the upside-down and backward-forward contrary women-men. Ours is the twisted road that forks back into itself. Ours is the angry coyote who knows peace. We have clowned you up and we will clown you out. Believe us or we will die as we must believe in you or you will die. We are the renegades of power. This medicine will live within you and work its magic."

"Hello, Lynn." Then I heard voices spoken in unison and echoing from cliff to cliff. The sound was threatening my ability for any cohesive thought, one word following another in a funeral parade of sound that left a wide scar in my perception. "Hello, Lynn. Hello, Lynn. Hello, Lynn."

I watched Agnes and Ruby die to their maleness as they slowly backed away from me and utterly disappeared into the darkness. Then I saw a blinding silvery light and I was hot with an implosive shock. I was catapulted backward; then somehow my trajectory turned around and threw me forward. I shot down a ribbed tunnel as if I were experiencing the mystery of conception and birth. The next thing I knew, I was kneeling on the ground within the circle with the bowl between my legs. I felt a gentle wind and I was slightly sick to my stomach. I got up with the bowl and left the circle as I had entered it. I knew I was no longer pregnant. I had given birth to myself. I went to the wall, crying. I began scraping at a reddened area with the scraping stick. The surface lit up like the light of dawn as I scraped. The tiny particles that fell in the bowl seemed to be part of the flesh of God—the substance of God.

I knew I was venturing into an inconceivable realm of ecstasy and pain that was rupturing my sensibilities. It was somehow mirrored in the beauty of the stone and my interaction with it. I touched it lovingly with my fingers. The smooth red surface softened and began to give away under the light pressure. It felt like elastic skin. As it loosened, something inside of me also gave away. I experienced my muscles snapping deep inside as if I were a musical instrument being unstrung and then restrung, to create a new harmony. I was getting closer to the core with each scraping of rock. All the theater and thoughts and false emotions I had been carrying were being flushed from my system. I knew suddenly that in bad sorcery and bad magic there is a reaction against love, and that this stone in its yielding, in its vulnerability, was teaching me something about caring. I felt in the mixture of rock, sound, emotions, and love, an alchemical distillation. I knew this was a death of my own destructive potential, because to have this experience I had let go of so much.

Tears were running down my face. I felt I was standing at a shrine of great meaning, and that somehow the God-substance cared for all things more than it was humanly possible to know. I sunk to my knees and wept with joy until I felt Agnes's hand rest on my shoulder.

Later, at the cabin, Agnes refused to discuss the vision with me. She said that discussing it would negate it, and that I should strive to carry the vision with me always. "At the very least," Agnes said, "you merged with evil and went through to love. Put the experience and the love into your shield." She said the east shield was a backward shield, that I should turn the face of it inward.

She said also the east shield was a formless shield and could be made any way that I saw fit, as long as it kept me conscious of the vision. She told me not to think of myself as I normally did, but to let the heyoka guides instruct me. I was to let my spirit make the shield. Agnes said that the heyoka shield wasn't really a shield at all, but the acknowledgment of the acceptance of spirit. "The heyoka shields that hang in museums have always been a mystery," she said. "Fantastic stories have been told of their powers—some true, some untrue. The heyoka shield seemed crazy to most non-Indians, something crude made by savages unable even to protect themselves. But when I see a heyoka shield, I know I am looking at something the ordinary person can't understand. What I see greets me, for I see the shield of a heyoka and I know great joy. It is a shield that says, 'I am not deceiving you. I have held council with the ridiculous. I am astonished at nothing, for I know that all things are but the will of the Great Spirit.' "

"If you won't talk about my vision, will you tell me what I am really doing when I make my heyoka shield?" I asked.

"You are trying to complete your circle."

"What does that mean?"

"Everyone is born belonging to a circle."

"I don't understand."

"There is no power until you have completed your circle."

"Do you mean a circle of people?"

"Yes. In your case, a circle of women. The task of the huntress, the task of the warrioress, is the gathering of enough personal power to be able to join with your circle once you find them."

"How do I do this?"

"You find your circle only when you are ready, and no one will ever succeed in this great and worthy struggle without being close to self-completion. Your circle has been calling you since the day of your birth. You have never had the personal power to hear them. You have confronted those in your circle many times in the past, but they were invisible to you. It is your responsibility never to doubt the existence of this sisterhood. Before you can enter and be recognized into your society, you must learn many things. When you join them, they give you gifts and their power becomes your power."

Agnes pointed me to my work, and wouldn't say another thing about the east shield. I remembered how a friend said to me once that when you see divinity, everything appears hysterically funny. I had a similar feeling while constructing the east shield. I kept looking at my strange collection of materials—the pile of cliff scrapings, the old mule hide, bent wood pieces, owl feathers, little plastic key chain tipis, a gourd rattle with no seeds in it, a hunting knife with a rusty, broken blade, several wooden trade nickels with Indian heads on them, to say nothing of chicken bones, and an old gnarled heyoka arrow with the point turned inward—and I was struck by the absurdity of the human dilemma. Putting the shield together, I would laugh for no apparent reason. Each step of the process seemed even more ludicrous, until I would suddenly laugh out loud. I knew it was admissible to do a sloppy job, and that too was wonderful. The shield began to look like a collection of Indian kitsch of the medicine world.

There seemed to be one important act in the order of events, and that was to figure out a way to use the scrapings from the heyoka barrier. Finally, using my own spit to mix it with, I worked the scrapings into the entire mule skin. I was just putting the last owl feather on the rim when Agnes appeared and plucked it out of my hand.

She smiled at me. "You never finish a heyoka shield. And now is a time to be especially careful. Remember that a heyoka shield attracts the enemy. It is an unfinished shield, but its power is immense and irresistable to those who understand it. Be sure of everything you do. And now you are securely on the path. You have been initiated into my heyoka world."

The next morning after I finished the shield, I drove into Crowley to get Ruby a few cartons of cigarettes. I bought them at the trading post, and then decided I would drive to a small town near the reserve and have a bite to eat. I also toyed with the idea of buying gifts for Agnes, Ruby, July, and even Ben and Drum. The local residents stared at me when I entered the community. I chalked it up to my being a stranger. I found myself curiously interested in the clean and comfortable-looking houses. The yards were neat and trim. Traffic was thin and the downtown area was only a couple of blocks long. I could have been driving in an average town anywhere. I parked and had a sandwich. When I came out of the cafe, I saw an old woman wrapped in an Indian blanket, her white hair tied in a knot. She was holding a stack of yellowed magazines.

After a moment, I recognized her as the woman I had seen in the trading post over in Crowley.

"Aren't you Phoebe?" I asked.

"Yes, I think I am." Phoebe was wearing the same print dress she had on the last time I saw her. The stack she was holding contained thirty or forty magazines. Her chin was wedged over a picture of Marilyn Monroe.

"Help me carry these," she said, handing me the stack. I had no other choice than to take them. I grabbed them before they fell to the sidewalk.

"My place is just a ways," she said.

I was getting irked. I felt that Phoebe was being fairly presumptuous to think I would cart her home. "I'm in a bit of a hurry."

"I am, too," she said, giving me a tiny nudge on the arm toward my car. I saw plainly enough then that I was going to have to take care of her. Phoebe went immediately to my car and got in the back seat. I wondered how she knew which one it was. I had to set the load of magazines on the hood in order to open the door, which she had shut. She made no attempt to help me as I stuffed the old magazines on the seat next to her. I got behind the wheel.

"Okay, where to, Phoebe?"

"You'll find it," she said. "Down the road."

I had no idea where I was going, and I got more exasperated by the minute. Phoebe began singing in a high, uneven voice. The song was nonsensical and seemed to be from the point of view of a child who was cutting out paper dolls. I wondered if she was retarded. I kept asking her if we were anywhere near her house. By now we had driven down every street in the town. Phoebe said no.

"Turn here," she said, pointing down a long tree-lined dirt road. About a mile and a half later, I pulled up to a decrepit house with a fallen-in shingled roof. The windows were all broken and boarded over.

"This place is deserted," I said. "You can't live here."

"I used to live here," Phoebe said.

"Come on, Phoebe. I don't care where you used to live. I have to get back to town. Please tell me where you live now."

She began singing again.

"Please, Phoebe." My head and arms were resting on the steering wheel. "Where do you live?"

She turned her head and looked at me as though absolutely nothing I had said had registered. She pointed down at one of the magazines that had fallen to the floor.

"I know you were sent here by my papers," she said, picking up the magazine and thumbing through it looking at the pictures.

"I think I've got the idea," I said. I turned the car around and drove back the way I had come. She was obviously demented, probably suffering from senile psychosis. I had just about decided to take her back to the town and drop her off where I had found her when she handed me a fan she had fashioned out of a page torn from the old magazine. The fan reminded me of Japanese origami work.

"For me? Thank you, Phoebe. I'll treasure it. But please, Phoebe, can't you remember where you live. Can't you show me the way?"

"Stop up there at that green house on the corner," she said. She flipped through the pages of a magazine.

I drove up to the house and parked without cutting off the engine. Phoebe jumped out and walked quickly through a picket fence gate, up the sidewalk, and into the house.

"Phoebe, wait a minute. What about your magazines?"

I cut the ignition and got out. I loaded up the magazines and hurried up the sidewalk. The front door was still open. I went on inside and sat the magazines down on a coffee table. I turned to leave. Instead, I stopped in my tracks. I faced Red Dog.

"I want to talk to you. Sit down."

A cold chill ran through me. I was too shocked to even contemplate how I had gotten into this situation. My eyes seemed to flicker and refuse to accept his presence. Red Dog closed the door and bolted it.

"Go on," he said. "Sit down. Make yourself at home."

I slid into a chair. Red Dog came over and looked down at me with a hard, unblinking stare, exhaling repressed fury with every breath. I knew he was ready to scratch out my eyes and thrust me blindly into the void.

He was wearing a sky-blue western shirt, jeans, and expensive wing-tipped cowboy boots. He didn't look as old as I remembered. There was a fire burning in the fireplace, and subtle shifts of color glistened on his close-fitting shirt. Much against my will, I began to tremble violently. I looked at his legs and glanced around the room for a wheelchair. He read my thoughts. "That wheelchair was just a decoy. Settle down, Lynn. Would you care for something to drink?" He was very sarcastic.

"Yes," I managed to say, knowing I wouldn't drink anything he gave me—but wanting time.

Red Dog went into the kitchen. My eyes darted around the room desperately, looking for an avenue of escape. There were locks on every door and window. The room was chaotic—a great jumble of plastic flowers, stacks of colored paper, newspapers, shelves of dolls (some old Indian dolls and some ordinary plastic dolls), and every kind of knickknack and bric-a-brac. There were many wind-up toys and building blocks, even a hamster in a red cage that continually ran on a treadmill. There was a cage with two parakeets that screeched every time one of the many cats wandered too close. Red Dog was soon back with what appeared to be iced wine and two glasses. My hands were shaking and the ice cubes were nearly rattling out of the glass. I was trying to appear unafraid, but the drink turned out to be raspberry Kool-Aid. I just sniffed the sugary smell.

"I don't approve of alcohol," he said, as though reading my mind again and greatly enjoying my obvious terror.

I sat the glass down on the coffee table. Phoebe brought in a plate of toasted peanut butter and jelly sandwiches. She sat them next to my drink and went over to an antique sewing machine and began to peddle away. Then she stopped and fanned herself frantically with one of the many old paper fans sitting on a table. The fans had

religious designs of Jesus, Mary, and Joseph. Red Dog paid her no
mind and took a sandwich.

"It's so hot," Phoebe complained. "These flies drive me crazy."

She began to pump the sewing machine again. As far as I could
tell, it was quite cold and there were no flies in the house. Also,
there was no thread or material in the sewing machine. With the
sound of the sewing machine, the hamster, the birds and cats, the
room sounded like an engine preparing for takeoff. Neither Phoebe
or Red Dog seemed to notice. I thought I had walked into bedlam
and wondered if I was going to be able to get out alive.

Red Dog leaned back in his chair and swallowed the last bite of
his peanut butter sandwich. "You know, your teachers have taught
you wrong, Lynn," he said.

"No, I don't know that."

Red Dog shook his head. "Dead wrong. They told you that I am
your enemy, yet you are no match for me. Why do you think they
are teaching you to shield yourself?"

"To become powerful."

Red Dog laughed derisively. "Nonsense. You are learning to
shield and gather power to protect yourself against me. Yet here I
am, and what could you do to prevent me from doing anything I
want? You see, I am not your nemesis. I have brought you here to
talk some sense into you. Don't be afraid of me." He took another
sandwich off the plate, examined it, and put it back.

"There's no way I am going to trust you."

I thought he was going to go into a towering rage, and I wished I
had kept silent.

"You stupid woman," he said. "Agnes taught you to be visible. Is
she visible? Is Ruby visible? Am I visible? Of course I can lead you
to them and they can lead you to me, but try finding any of us if we
don't want you to. I look at you with pity. Visibility is your nemesis.
A true person of power blends into the background—you can't see
them. That's how they retain what they have. You have bid for
power and you are finding it and perhaps you will be just like me.
That is the most lonely of conditions. You are a white woman who

does not fit anywhere, just like me. Most of the Native world does not understand you. Agnes has led you through magic, and you can never again take part in the mass dream. What are you going to do now? Where are you going to go?"

"I'll go back home and lead my life as I normally do."

Red Dog lifted his hand as though to block what I said. "No one will recognize you. They'll put the screws to you to get you to conform and behave like that person they once knew. You won't be able to utilize your knowledge because if you do, they will become afraid of you. In your power they will only experience the lack of their own. They will not see that you have changed and will not know who you are. You will spend your time seeking your circle. Do you think you will ever find your sisters? Of course not. Not all the shields in the world can give you the sisterhood, because the sisterhood does not exist. If the sisterhood existed, don't you think I would know about it? I would steal their power. But I have always had to contain my female power in the form of sacred objects like the marriage basket. I have sought the world over to find a woman who could give me the power I seek. None have ever proved worthy. And will you find a real man? Right now I have Phoebe's power. Don't underestimate her. She is enormously strong."

"Phoebe?" I couldn't imagine Red Dog with that strange little old lady. "What on earth kind of power could she have?"

"Her paper brought you here. She could kill you this moment. You see, I don't want to kill you because I want you to have power. To destroy you now would dishonor me because you're so weak and stupid. Phoebe, come over here a moment. I want you to smoke Lynn. I want you to look into her and tell me what you see."

Phoebe came over from the sewing machine. She was humming and she bent down and looked into my face in a demented way. "The woman in the mirror, she thought she was, a mere woman in time. Her voice asked what was reflected there, what was reflected there, where she stood, she understood, behind her was the form of things and a house and the corner where the mouse watched things that were the forms. Each thing and form shouted a question from the reflection of time in the mirror within the house. Constructed forms cast their shadows and reflected the light of atoms of substance, but there was no romance of the night nor play and very little to say . . . by the woman named Lynn in what had been made or not much said about the maiden that once was. The mirror reflected her mind and the furniture of her thinking, never blinking because all was from the past, nothing would last. She moved around her furniture and in among her goods, never thinking once of what she understood, polishing the table and not able to find that perfect rule that would measure her abilities. Such humility! And how cruel the fool that did not say what she wanted the fool to say that day. If only the reflection were part of the perfection she dreamed would be, just you wait and see. If only! If only! Oh, how the child grew. She flew marking the notes in an old-fashioned drama that graded her peers. It lasted so many years, so many, how? Tired, moving among clutter and spreading the bread with the butter. Why should I putter when there is something to do? Wouldn't you? I will write it, paint it, do for you for you! For me there is no time and no rhyme or reason, nothing pleasing except for my pride, why hide? I am without blame . . . no shame, a model mother, what other? In the mirror waiting, waiting, waiting for the day I will have something to say."

Red Dog cut her off. "That's quite enough, Phoebe. Perhaps Lynn realizes that you see her better than she thought."

Phoebe's sing-song words had caused me to shiver. She went over to a shelf that was filled with old, round cardboard hat boxes.

"Where did I leave my scissors?" she said, lifting the tops to the boxes and rummaging through the contents. "Oh, here they are." She brought out a pair and held them up to the light, clicking them. "I don't like the way that white lady looked at me yesterday in the store."

Red Dog watched her carefully. "Why don't you bob her tail, Phoebe. Why don't you fold her arms on her chest and lower her into the ground?"

"Yes, the woman in the store will find the door to no-more. I'll paper her to the grave for what she gave." She pulled some black, heavy paper out of one of the hat boxes. She began cutting it with the scissors and it began to take the form of a paper doll with hands held up next to its head, fingers outstretched. Then she cut out eyes and a mouth in diamond shapes. She added a black skirt above the knees, then she cut out two legs with feet spread out and big pointed toes. She held it up for Red Dog to see.

"She is cut out of black paper to make her sick," cried Phoebe.

I didn't have the slightest idea what they were doing, but I suspected that something diabolically evil was about to happen. I didn't dare ask any questions. Some potent force around the two of them was turning black. Phoebe was now cutting out a rectangular shape from some brown paper and she laid the black doll on top of it like it was lying on a bed. She started to chant in an Indian tongue and Red Dog left the room, a glint of pleasure in his eye. He soon returned with some pungent smoking incense.

The malignant conjuring continued. They placed the paper doll and the bed on a small altar next to the wall. Phoebe hummed to herself as she placed plastic flowers and chocolate cigarettes, and lit candles. Again and again she passed the doll through the smoke from the incense. Red Dog handed her a small vial of red fluid that appeared to be blood. Phoebe sprinkled it on the doll. She then took a pod that was shaped like a tiny bull horn (it may have been acacia) and thrust it through the doll where her stomach would be. Time and again she would blow her breath into the doll and chant. I watched in horror. The procedure was incredible. So this is what Red Dog was doing with this woman. He was learning some vile form of black magic. There was so much dreadful power around this little old lady that it crackled. In her eccentric innocence, Phoebe had tapped into a great evil reservoir and was wielding it with the emotional maturity of a seven-year-old.

I couldn't stand it anymore and started to move towards the kitchen—maybe there was an open door. Red Dog leapt up and shoved me back into my chair. He nodded his approval to Phoebe, still watching me. Then Phoebe rolled up all the offerings, the doll, and other items, and told him to go get a shovel so he could bury her and be finished with her. Phoebe's face was contorted with anger. Her eyes stabbed at me once with the kind of black power that only an irrational hatred can find. I felt shriveled up inside.

As I witnessed this horrible ritual, I realized that Red Dog, in his obsession for power, was really quite mad. In his delusion, he was seeing what he thought was himself in me. Because he had never developed the female side in himself, he couldn't see me clearly. I thought maybe I could escape this crazy man alive—if I could just play as vulnerable and stupid as I felt and as weak as he said I was.

Red Dog went outside and presumably buried the material they had just used. He returned and sat in the flowered, overstuffed chair near the fireplace. Phoebe left the room and didn't return. Red Dog turned his attention on me.

"You may wonder what happened to Phoebe. When she was young, she took up with a very bitter sorcerer. He wasn't a nice person like me. She soon tired of him and when she tried to leave him, he left her with the mind of a child. Now she works her sorcery that he taught her from the south in her simple trust and innocence. She still has the power that he taught her and more, but she is a woman whose memories and history belong only to her forgotten lover. I guess you can see we are nobody to be fooling around with," he finished, swaggering a bit in his chair. A cat at his feet yowled and leapt away. To me they were conjuring the earth's destruction, both fugitives from love, thrust into a lonely abyss. Life to them was confusion, struggle, and revenge, the mark of pain upon our sacred dream.

I looked at him and began to sob uncontrollably into my hands.

"Well, I'm glad to see that you're aware of your precarious state. Hell, that paper stuff is only first grade. I could do a lot worse than that if I wanted to."

I pretended I couldn't stop crying. He handed me a blue bandana to blow my nose.

"Goddam it, stop that sniveling. Some medicine woman you are."

"I can't help it. I'm so frightened."

"What are you afraid of? Certainly not me. You're no kind of challenge," he sneered. "Look at you. It will take you years to be ready for me. I'm much too dangerous for you to take on again. Without Agnes, you're nothing."

Now I was completely unable to control myself or quit sobbing.

"I'm going to let you go. I hadn't really planned to, but I've

decided I am. Now quit that blubbering. Here. I'll tell you what.
I'm going to make you a little gift to make you feel better."

If I had not been so terrified, I would have been suspicious of his
docile behavior. Red Dog got Phoebe's scissors and began to cut out
a very beautiful circular design, not unlike a snowflake with wavy
patterns in it. He was using black paper and he worked very quickly.
He put the finished piece on my lap and said, "Here. This
represents the spirit of the air. Give it to Agnes and tell her that I
menace the two of you with every breath that you take. Now get
back to your precious teacher. If I ever catch you dogging me again,
Phoebe will look like Albert Einstein compared with what's left of
you."

I got the hell out of that madhouse as fast as I could. Somehow, I
managed to drive back to the Reserve and find my way to Agnes's
cabin. I was still crying as I ran down the path toward the house.
Agnes was sitting out front with all my shields around her. She
called out for me to stop and not to come any closer.

"I've been sending you power. I knew you were in great danger.
The power of the heyoka shield attracted you to him. You have
something that is really meant for me. What is it?"

"I have a paper cutout that is in the shape of a snowflake. That's
all I have."

"That's some of Red Dog's sorcery that contains the seeds of harm
for me. He has totally tricked you. His gift would have killed me.
That's his way of destroying you. Take it out of sight of the cabin.
Tear it to pieces and bury it in four separate places and then return
quickly."

I did as she said. Then I ran back to Agnes and nearly fell on her
sobbing with relief and terror. I told her everything that had
happened. She kept stroking my back and then she started to laugh.
I pulled away and looked at her with alarm.

"Why are you laughing?"

"You also tricked him. You did it. Your vulnerability is your best
shield. You were so wide open that he couldn't see your power. You
blinded him with your innocence."

"Then why am I building these shields?"

"Don't mistake it. These shields saved you because they represent your power. They define you and your strength. Sometime soon you will learn to put them together and use them as a whole. Red Dog let you go because he's deranged. He thinks you are just like him, that you need someone outside yourself for power. But you don't. He thinks everyone wants to be a sorcerer. Oh, this is too good." Agnes was fairly screeching with laughter. "You're a good apprentice. I think you're free of him for awhile."

I wiped away my tears and smiled, and then I had to laugh, too. We spoke of the incident until after dinner, Agnes giving me an inordinate amount of affection and care. She knew that I needed it.

The next day I decided to walk over to Ruby's rather than drive. I needed the exercise to ground me. I started out with a knapsack containing the cigarettes and my newly "unfinished" shield. I felt pretty unsettled and I had a running dialogue with myself all the way there. I was still very shaken and depressed about my encounter with Red Dog. He had said a lot of things very well. Even though I knew that he saw reality in a twisted way, his words had made me less sure of my decisions. The visions I had at the heyoka barrier, though rewarding had also been very confusing. Had I really seen Agnes and Ruby as young men? I sure thought I had. And what did it mean to me and my life in Los Angeles? I understood that the world is not as it seems and that most of us have everything all backwards, but what was I going to do, reverse my activities and behave in a way that would be nonsensical and idiotic to everyone in my life back home? I remembered the first time I had come back from Canada. It had been very difficult for me because I couldn't explain anything about my experiences. My daughter had felt left out, and my friends had been confused by my remoteness. I had found it enormously difficult to go back to paying bills and earning a living, to say nothing of playing social games. Understanding this heyoka path was even more difficult. I couldn't figure out how to apply this philosophy to myself. So I resolved to get some answers from Ruby when I showed her the backward shield. I supposed that was what Agnes wanted me to do, since she refused to give me any

explanation. Then again, perhaps Agnes wanted me to come to the
answers in my own time. As a result, I was feeling depressed and
uncertain. I really needed to clear my head. I kept seeing those
awful paper cutouts of Phoebe's. Had all this really happened?

When I reached Ruby's, the sky was overcast and a slight breeze
moved the tree tops. Ruby was standing in the doorway, drying her
hands on a towel.

"Hi, Ruby. I'm here."

"I figured you were. You have the shield, don't you?"

"Yes," I said, holding it out to her as if I were proferring the
moon. Ruby took it and immediately gave me one of her big,
satisfied grins. I had so rarely seen that expression on her face that
for a moment she looked like a stranger.

"Ho," she said, "this is quite a shield, Lynn."

She investigated every inch of it carefully. By holding the palm of
her hand above the face of the shield, she was able to know the
colors I used and comment on them. She read me the shield in
detail. I was never more impressed with her ability to see without
eyes than at that moment.

"Where is July? And Ben and Drum?" I said as an afterthought.

"I have sent them each on a different journey. They will be back
Monday, in three days. They have gone for the weekend." Ruby
motioned for me to come in and sit down at the table. She placed
the shield between us with great care. Then she did something most
unusual for her. She scooted her chair around to sit beside me. "I
just want to be a little closer to you," she said. "It helps me to see
you better. What I am going to say is important. Don't write
anything down. Just hear me. I will try to brush away your
confusion. I know this is a very hard time for you."

She lit a cigarette and held it up briefly. I knew it was her way of
praying.

"I want to put you on the right road," she said finally. "And the
right road is where all roads merge. There are many faces on the
heyoka path. Your heyoka face is an unusual one. Humanity usually
knows the heyoka as a beggar, clown, coyote, fool, trickster. Agnes
has told me of the stories you have told her of the Buddha. If I

understand correctly, the Buddha was a great heyoka." Ruby had gone into a trancelike state and was more articulate than I thought she was capable of being, although her English was still rough.

"First, there's the Grandfather Sun, who was young once and is now a grandparent of great powers, but the sun will one day go into the void. And that's the power of the heyoka—the void.

"Lynn, what do you believe in?"

"I just try to stay present."

"Hmm. Do you remember who you are?"

"Well, yes," I said, not sure what she meant. She went on.

"Heyoka respects no ritual, philosophic system, or belief. History is contained within this power. To take you into history and make you live it is a heyoka power. To become Crazy Horse or George Washington. It's the power of death—corruption of the body by flame and going back to earth. In woman, man, or vice versa, the heyoka has been the great lover of children, healing them and protecting them. To someone who is not part of this tradition, a heyoka Indian will seem to work in strange ways. Heyoka people will come and beg for food during ceremonies. The medicine woman wouldn't dare bother them, because a heyoka has the power to destroy the ritual. He is the disturber of ritual, the trickster, he tests your beliefs to see if they're real. To be a heyoka you have to be enlightened—being a heyoka makes you a backward woman or man because you see the reflection of life, like you saw by walking and holding a mirror.

"I want to give you a meditation, one that was given to me a long time ago.

"Imagine you're leaning over a pool of water—the first mirror. You dive into the water and your reflection comes up to meet you. What happens to your reflection on the plane of the surface of the pool? Think a minute.

"You can see that's a kind of crossroads—if you can unravel that, you can go beyond the crossroads. It's just another symbol. Going beyond what's known into White Buffalo Woman, to you that would be the unknown. You have true death in enlightenment—this is one of many mysteries. The end is where seven roads fork the dream.

Choose one of the roads if you want power, or you can run back and say 'I've gone too far.' When you look down you see seven auras—pick up crooked, twisted arms of heyoka and know love and trust.

"A heyoka has the power of hot and cold. She can reach into bubbling hot meat in a kettle and, taking it, she can eat it without being burned. The world has a powerful need for understanding this way because it's the power of void, of woman. Men teach women—women, men. No other Native tradition teaches the opposite sex. We need to heal the woman in us all.

"We're like the water. Heyoka has to do with primal eroticism that comes from the beginnings of life, from your cells. Our cells contract and expand and produce regeneration and life. We, as life forms, reproduce this effect in love and in knowledge. Sometimes we use plants to break through a mind barrier into the inner lodges. This is so that the phenomenon of expansion and contraction can be understood in love. Because the heyoka has to do with love. It's the womb, the void. If we're the lake—as I see you in me—I'm in you. We're the great mirror. We're nothing but the reflection of each other. If I didn't have anybody around, I would only have myself to define myself.

"Black holes in the universe are symbols. Everything is backward to itself in a heyoka vision. Life is bad, death is good, because we've been tricked into our own illusions. The way has to do with the paradox of life—I love you means I hate you on some level. Do you understand?" She didn't wait for my answer.

"Do you remember that dream you had about me? When you thought you were seeing into my head—a tapestry behind me—those knots you saw were my heyoka teachers. You can be easily confused by a heyoka into thinking they are black magicians, because they deal with the void—death and rebirth. But they are not. One reason this medicine is so powerful is because it's the destroyer of heroes. Heroes fear the heyoka, because the heyoka can see through them, can see their feet of clay. People who define themselves only by themselves often are powerful, but they have no womb. They need wombness to be sisters and brothers over and over.

"I can walk through a gathering and snake them into confusion—I can get inside your head and turn you around, and you don't know what you're doing. If I can confuse you, then you know you must get stronger. My life is a teaching. I stay in the simple because it's the most sensible. I'm not bragging. It's just what is. The heyoka will always take a new and different step. I'm sure it sounds strange, but this is the most powerful way if you can understand it. It is a way of beauty and love. They say that a heyoka remembers the trail and takes a different one. So? If you meet a heyoka, you want to shut your eyes and quickly walk by, because any confrontation will change your life forever." She stopped talking, felt my hand for a moment, and then read my mind.

"I know that still doesn't fully explain their odd behavior. They come from this idea—heyoka is an awake one—they walk backward because they know God is behind them. Trust and fall backward—they know the Great Spirit will catch them. They make you see yourself and your illusions. They dance the peace dance in a time of war."

Then Ruby turned in her chair and planted a big kiss on my cheek. I almost fell off my chair in surprise.

"Now rest for awhile while I go pray over your shield." She left and I lay down on her bunk bed. All of what she had said rung true and danced through my mind. I felt much better and less confused. How I had come to love that old woman!

Shield-Made-of-Shadows: Self

The moon by arrangement
grows full, begins in
returning us our night vision.

Cycles we follow.
Anticipations we chase
lost on a future ship
not yet sea worthy.

Stars are no longer lights
and fists in the sky carry
earth's anger. There is no
walking away.

If in sight of the moon
we can free our eyes from their
fixed positions

here
the possibilities of distance
open in the remaining seas.

Without easing
aloneness
we come to be where we are.

Life is fragile.
Our pieces are connected
to the same puzzle.

—JACK CRIMMINS, from
*Thread the Silence
Like a Needle*

I cleaned the dishes from the table and wiped it thoroughly. Agnes put her hand on mine. The skin of her tapering fingers felt thin and slippery like the underbelly of a lizard. We looked at each other for a long moment.

"There are elk feeding behind the cabin," she said. She looked away. "They are not content. This land is not the happy place it once was." I looked sharply at Agnes, for I was unused to hearing a sad tone in her voice. Her mood had suddenly shifted.

"I'm terribly sorry," I said. "For the animals, I mean. I feel it, too."

Agnes was motionless, as though her thoughts were miles away. I thought tears might be rolling down her cheeks. But when she turned to me her eyes were transformed with a girlish twinkle, a coyote's gaze under aging, wrinkled lids. I stepped back from the table into the night shadows that were forming.

"We have all changed," she said, motioning with her hand as though she were smoothing something. "I think we understand each other."

She unbuttoned the pocket of her Pendleton shirt. Inside was a small medicine bag, which she brought out and handed to me. I took it and held it tightly, feeling the edges of the crystal inside.

Agnes said, "You should have a snake and live with it. You will give away power to each other."

"A snake?" I stammered.

"Yes, rattlesnakes are a good protection for women."

"But I really wouldn't feel good about living with a snake."

"You didn't feel good about living with me, either. You would get used to living with a sister rattlesnake, too. It is not that different."

Agnes would often do this, vaguely confuse me before I went off into the night to face what I thought was yet another life-and-death situation. I had the feeling she was trying to rattle me. She had frightened me pretty well in the past to make me vulnerable to something new. Tonight I couldn't even look at her. There was something odd about the way she moved and looked at me. I just wanted to get away and start up my mountain. I stacked my four shields on top of each other and put my medicine bundle on top of that, then I held them against my stomach. We went outside.

"The moon's up in the east. A star is out, a magical star that tells me all is ready." Agnes pointed to a tiny star that didn't look too important among so many others. It was just over the trees in the distance. But she sounded like Tonto speaking to the Lone Ranger. "Some Indians call that star the star-that-calls-the-dolphins-from-the-sea."

"You sound like Tonto," I said, a bit annoyed.

"I am completely serious. That star is awesome." She made several jerky gestures with her shoulders and then, taking my arm in hers, danced me up the trail to my car.

"I'll drive," Agnes said. She started to climb in behind the wheel while I was putting the shields in the back.

"Agnes, you aren't going to frighten me to death. Besides, I don't think I have insurance for you. Please let me drive."

"After tonight, you won't need any insurance." She slowly slid over to the other side of the seat. "Machines like this take your energy. Go ahead and drive."

I kept thinking about Agnes and her off-handed behavior as we drove in silence. I felt about as sacred as my car. I had thought that this ceremony I was doing tonight was to be the most important of all. Sometimes nothing made any sense. Then I remembered an experience I had with Agnes years ago. I had dysentery and had been hallucinating. I had looked at Agnes, and suddenly I had realized that knowledge is a kind of wall that has to be torn down in order to experience illumination. I saw the great simplicity of it all and I laughed. I had turned a difficult corner on my path, and I laughed all that day and the next day as well. It was so obvious and yet so elusive. Each time the realization came back to me, I laughed out loud. A teacher keeps you from the very thing you are looking for. And what is truth? asked Pontius Pilate, washing his hands.

And now as we drove down a completely deserted road toward the grey mountains in the night, Agnes giggled as if she knew what I was thinking. We both laughed until tears flooded our cheeks. Then we were silent again, except for her periodic directions to turn left or right on various hard-to-see gravel roads. Our humor had somehow made me feel strong, and I felt balanced. I had let go of vanity—a little bit of the mass dream.

We drove up a long series of switchbacks and then Agnes leaned
forward abruptly and told me to pull in to the left over by a dark
stand of trees and stop. We got out of the car and I got my shields.
This area in the hills was totally unfamiliar to me. A slight mist
seemed to roll downward from the top of the mountain, moving
around a jumble of great boulders. The longer I stared at them the
higher they seemed to get. Agnes told me to set my shields down on
the hood of the car for a moment and come with her. She led me
over to the base of a massive, dark-colored rock. She took out her
tobacco pouch and handed me some tobacco. We placed the
tobacco offerings on a flat rock for the spirit of the mountain. After
this formality, Agnes told me to get my shields, wrap them in a
blanket, and follow her. She indicated a hidden trail that wound up
between the rocks at a very steep incline. I scrambled along behind
Agnes as we began our ascent. I was slipping and sliding with every
step, balancing my shields as best I could. I was almost on all fours
at times. The trail was very difficult, and much further than I
expected. Finally, we reached the top. I sat down next to Agnes in
the dirt, panting, trying to catch my breath. The new moon was
barely a sliver in the star-filled sky, and yet it was enough to cause
two or three coyotes to yap at it like young pups. The coyote barking
was coming from the west and I looked carefully around me. The
mountaintop consisted of a large flat surface about one hundred
yards across. There were three distinct piles of rocks in a pyramidal
shape. A great barren distance stretched in all directions around us,
broken only by the stacks of rocks. I walked over to one of the
pyramids. It was covered by a mosslike growth and felt ancient and
glued together from the passage of the ages. Now that I was getting
my bearings, I noticed there was a large circle of stones all around
us and that the three pyramidal piles were in the center of the circle
or just slightly above the center. I realized that I was standing in the
middle of a giant, ancient medicine wheel. I turned to Agnes and
shivered as the powerful emanations of the mountaintop began to
work on me.

"Grandfather Mountain is very old," Agnes said. "He was very
sacred to the ancestors. He will be here a long time and he has seen

many things. Always show respect and honor by giving him tobacco before you come here. He calls out to many kinds of power and many kinds of power answer him. Here, within the ancient wheel, many new powers are born. This circle is the earthly shield of the sky beings. May their four winds blow gently on you for all the years to come. May they illuminate your shields."

We were silent for a moment, and then Agnes helped me spread out my blanket a few yards to the south of the three pyramidal shapes. It took a while to satisfy Agnes. She swept away old pebbles and twigs. She indicated that I should sit on the blanket.

"What should I expect tonight?" I asked.

"There is no way to tell," Agnes said. "You may see the shining mountain spirit and be led on incomprehensible journeys. You may see a magical bird or coyote or dog. You may magically fly to Sskuan and never come down from this sacred mountain. You are now the perfect reflection of these three pyramids above you." She pointed at them. "As above, so below. The important thing is to be serious, to be attentive, to let your knowing be balanced with substance. The medicine wheel is the perfect form for all content. It is form. In the beginning was Wakan, and Wakan is the great void. She is the great circle. She is everything—good, bad, time, space, the total of all things mixed as one. Then came Sskuan, the lightning bolt of illumination. He illuminated Wakan to both of her sides. He is the great mirror. Wakan looked within and found her man. Then they married and danced and became one, the sun. How can we speak of it? Up here, we have crossed over to another land, the land of the sky beings. Everything is changed here, everything is behind us, everything is different and contradictory."

Agnes began to sing softly, her face raised like a wolf to the sliver of moon. There was a pressure across the back of my shoulders, as if the stones of the ancient medicine wheel were trying to press in on me. The pyramids seemed to glow, first grey and then strangely white.

"Before I leave you, I want to smoke the pipe with you here on Grandfather Mountain," Agnes said. Then she told me how to take out my pipe. I laid out the contents of my medicine bundle and tied

Agnes's medicine bag to my waist. We smoked to the grandparents, the four directions, mother earth and sky father. The bowl glowed red, and shimmering plumes of smoke lifted from it. We offered our prayers and smudged ourselves with sweet grass. When we were finished I separated my pipe and put it away, offering the tobacco to the stones as there were no trees around.

"Remember to hold your attention," Agnes said, reaching over and taking my hands. She curled my fingers in toward my palms. "Whatever happens, keep centered and work with the energy here tonight. Don't try to name anything. Don't limit your perception and lose it. Everyone who has visited here has had ability, or power would have blocked their way. You are an ambassador of power. Do not be overwhelmed or frightened, or you may be snatched away from me. If you are still in this world and have not been taken away, come down the mountain at dawn. I will be waiting. If you do not come down, I will know that you have made your gift to power, and here our paths sever." She pressed against me in a brief hug and then withdrew into the night's shadows. I could hear an occasional rock breaking loose as she climbed down the trail.

With Agnes gone, I felt a rush of panic. It was uncanny how her presence made almost any situation tolerable. What had she meant, "taken away"? Suddenly, I was aware of the pyramids of stone. Then the strange idea occurred to me that they were three companions and I was the fourth. I wished I had asked Agnes about them before she left. Emanations from the medicine wheel seemed to push in on me, and I was very careful with my movements. I smoothed my hair back from my eyes. Then I realized I had done so quite rashly. Primordial forces dwelled here, and a false move would not be tolerated. The large rocks at the outer circumference of the wheel seemed to be breathing and getting larger.

I began to pray. I heard the coyotes howling again, or perhaps it was the howling wind in the distance. The rock beneath the blanket began to feel cold. Carefully, I unwrapped my four shields and placed them in their four directions around me. I was proud as I did this. I concentrated on the symbolism that I had put into each shield. My dreams and visions were an aspect of the very form and fabric of which they were built. The shields stood for the concept of who I am in my completeness. Together, they were the ultimate medicine wheel, the map from my outer to my inner being. To conceive of them was to conceive the mystery of my oneness. I had never set them out before. I was overwhelmed by their beauty and the manner in which they made me perceive myself. They were my very personification. The fifth shield was me, the void, the grandmother, the self. I sat in front of my south shield and I sang her song of trust and innocence. I repeated this in front of each shield, prayed and sang in front of the west for good medicine dreams and the rebirth of my spirit. I prayed and sang to the north for understanding and wisdom to fulfill my dreams and visions. Then to the heyoka east shield, I asked and sang for illumination. I made offerings of tobacco to each shield and then I smoked the pipe again in the center, the place of the Rainbow Chiefs, the seat of the invisible shield where all knowledge and spirit come together to secure form and direction. I stretched both my hands to the sky. Agnes had taught me to open myself at this point in the ceremony and to hold an image of my shields as parts of a shattered mirror fitted at once together to make a whole. I held this image and it became more and more visible and larger and larger in my mind, and then the broken mirror completed again, all woven and interlaced through time and my experience into a fabric of illusory substance called life, which when heated evaporates into metaphor and must in due time be distilled down through care into a new form once again. Then I knew it must be conveyed to another, then others—written on the wind in the four directions of the heart.

Suddenly, I heard the most incredible cracking noise somewhere in my back or head and the mirrored wheel began to whirl around me, in me, like a multicolored whirlpool sucking me into itself. It was as if I were sucked into myself and then turned inside out, like a fetus. The whole sky seemed to be filled with flashing lights—red, gold, white, blue. My back arched involuntarily as a great wind hit me, and I was thrown flat on my back as if a great weight were pressing down on me. I could feel the ground under my blanket turning hot and undulating in a vibrating rhythm. Now there were spinning silver things above me in the air and more lights became visible, lights everywhere coming out of the black sky. I couldn't move.

I fought with every ounce of strength I had to get to my feet. There was such a great wind that my hair was being yanked by it. I thought that my shields had been lifted up with me, off the flat surface of the plateau. They were approximately shoulder level or above. Certainly, they were going to blow away, but I could not move to save them. They seemed to turn amazingly fast. I thought for a moment I was standing in a different place. My shields were separating now and there were several shields, enormously enlarged and spinning above me. It was impossible to judge their distance. Lights flickered off the shields into the night. There were many hovering over me at different levels. I stared unblinking at this phenomenon. A beam of light fell on me; then another beam, in a circle. The light seemed to vibrate at an incredibly high frequency. It was jamming my mind and making me dizzy. I began to lose consciousness, and then everything shot out of sight.

The next thing I knew, it was dawn. I was laying flat on my back. I gingerly moved my aching head to look around. I wasn't sure exactly where I was. My shields were gone. I went around the circle and looked beyond the pyramids of rocks. I wondered if they had been blown down the mountain. Then I wondered if my shields had actually flown off into space. What an incredible dream I had had. I felt a little bit sunburned and I couldn't imagine how this could have happened to me during the night.

I rolled up my blanket and packed my things together. I was feeling very good. I ran and slid and tripped my way down the mountain. I hastened to get down to Agnes. I needed an explanation. I wanted her to explain exactly what had happened. My brain was bursting with incredulity.

She was sitting on the hood of the car with a blanket wrapped around her shoulders. Her face was very serious and she turned to see me coming, pulling the blanket even tighter around her.

"Agnes, I can't believe what has happened."

"I know. You've seen much. I want you to eat while you tell me of your experiences. I have brought a little food we can share. I believe you are hungry." Even if I am scared to death, I can usually eat something, and I was glad Agnes had thought to bring provisions.

We went over and sat under the branches of a pine tree. Between hurried bites of food, I told her everything and then begged for an explanation.

"They have taken your shields," she said. "I touch the earth in gratitude. You saw the flying sky shields."

"Who's they?"

"The flying shields. What you saw is called the Flight of the Seventh Moon."

"Do you mean my shields were flying around? Really?"

"No, Lynn. The sky beings came down to honor you and your shields. They came because you had the power to call them."

I was silent for a long time.

"Do you mean those flying shields are something like flying saucers?"

"Listen to me—I'll tell you a story from the ancient medicine belts. A long time ago, the medicine wheels were in outer space. They were beautiful and had every power except one. They could not touch. The medicine wheels looked down and they saw Mother Earth. They saw many creatures who could touch but had no feeling. The medicine wheels said to one another, 'Why don't we go down and enter into those creature's bodies so that their egos can feel and so the medicine wheels can touch. Look, down there are all those creatures walking around who cannot know each other.' So the medicine wheels went down and filled those creatures' bodies. When the medicine wheels come down it is called conception. At conception the medicine light becomes brilliant and then chooses a color. I always know when a women has conceived—because of the large and small lights. Power has entered her body. At death the medicine wheel returns to outer space and the earthbound body returns to Mother Earth.

"We are two beings and we are women. At this time our bodies and the wheels reside together. If we are dumb, the 'I' still wants to be boss. The 'I' doesn't care who it hurts as long as it gets what it wants. We have to use the 'I' to learn our lessons on our earth walk," Agnes said. "Our medicine wheel creates feeling and sentiments to give us balance."

Now I was really silent. I didn't say another word. When we reached the cabin, I went straight to bed, even though it was the middle of the day. I had always thought that UFO's and extraterrestrial talk were nonsense. I kept thinking that I must have been hallucinating, but Agnes had said that we had only smoked red willow bark.

I had a very disturbed sleep. I slept through to the morning of the next day, and even then I got up slowly. I had heard a strange thrumming noise and seen the multicolored lights in my confused dreams. I told Agnes about it, and she explained that our bodies and minds are like antennae and radio receivers. I asked her if she meant that we could receive AM and FM frequencies.

"Yes, those AM and FM currents are in the air around us all our lives, but we are never aware of them until we learn to tune our senses or radios and then we can be tuned to many worlds that live right along with us, AM and FM and many others unknown to our usual states of being. Some people have a certain amount of crystal in them. They are like radio receivers. The information is there for everybody. We are like antennae. Some of us are finely tuned. The knowledge is there for everybody. Life can really be difficult for people who have that crystal inside because they see so much."

I told Agnes that I felt disoriented because of the loss of my personal shields.

"Yes, I see some of the anxiety is with you. You do not remember even how long you were on the mountain. It might have been one night or even a week. How do you know?"

It was true that I had lost track of the exact dates since I had visited Agnes. I did, however, know the approximate date.

"It had to be one night," I said adamantly. "You waited for me."

"Lynn, you have entered the womb of the great mystery. You saw many things that you will remember only slowly because it is still beyond your personal power to know. You have come again from that great womb. Through that birth you will know the great mystery, for you are of it. You are the child of that mystery and from that birth comes the deathless life. You will remember the details as you begin to identify with the void that is woman. In you and in man, you sit in the center of the self shield in the place of the grandmothers. You gave up your lies. We all live a lie until we are reborn through the void. And when you remember it all, you will be a shaman woman who shows others that there is no death."

I felt such melancholy that I was crying. Or was I happy? I didn't know. Agnes put her arms around me and let me be. She made my weeping less. I looked out through the irregular glass windows to the autumn trees. There would be very few warm days ahead.

"Do you feel up to a picnic?" she asked.

"Sure, where?" I said, drying my eyes.

"You'll like it. It's very beautiful. Make some sandwiches."

We were on our way in thirty minutes, bouncing down the dirt road and singing loudly. The song was about wild turkeys and a mole. We made up the verses as we drove.

"Oh, what a magnificent lake," I said, parking my car. My depression had evaporated.

"Yes, the river joins the lake over there," she said, pointing from the front seat. Mist swirled over the white capped surface of the water and rose up in gnarled tufts. Agnes continued, "We are going to canoe up river about two miles."

We walked down a path through the rushes and out on a small, pebbly finger where a canoe was beached.

"I've never seen a real birchbark canoe before," I said, surprised at the discovery. I helped Agnes flip it over and thrust it out into the water. "Where did you get this?"

"I've had it a long time. Some Indian friends of mine made it for me. I hope you know how to paddle. The currents are not very strong."

"I used to have a canoe at Lake Arrowhead in California," I said. "I can manage."

"Let's go then." We put our blankets and food inside a basketlike enclosure at the center and carefully climbed aboard. Agnes pushed off and then cut into the water with quick, clean strokes of the paddle. Black waves dashed against the sides as we turned toward the mouth of the river. It was silent and cool. A heavy mist was moving through the pines and settled down over us. The experience was dreamlike, the mist first clearing and then sweeping around us in the canoe. Shafts of sunlight burst through the greyness. The water had calmed and was like oiled slate. The sound of our paddles was muffled and rhythmic. Soon we were pulling upstream on the river.

I giggled to myself.

"What are you laughing at?" Agnes asked.

"I was just thinking," I said. "This is a real good metaphor for my life—paddling upstream in a fog."

"I heard a better one, only it was without a paddle," Agnes said.

"That too," I agreed, laughing heartily.

As the mist settled, the air was moist and cold and I pulled my parka around my throat. The water stirred in foamy eddies with each stroke. It was fairly steady going. The current was lazy and slow. I caught sight of a sunny patch of beach around a tranquil bend in the river.

"How about there?" I asked.

"Not safe," Agnes said brusquely. "Indian country."

So we paddled ever further, but I felt happy and strong and as though I could go on forever. Crows cawed close overhead, trailing blue-grey shadows over the water. Now and again I would glimpse the unveiled sky. I felt swallowed in an immense, otherworldy scene. Agnes began to backpaddle.

She said, "Have you ever noticed how much faster we can go when we paddle together? Look what happens to the canoe when I work against you." We started to pitch and tip dangerously. "That is the difference between white women and Indian women who follow the old way. In your society, women get together in little groups and fight against each other instead of giving one another power and direction. It is a great tragedy for the world that your women don't have clans and traditions. With the support of other women you can do practically anything."

The canoe was fishtailing in a circle.

"Come on, Agnes. I'm starving."

In answer, Agnes leveled out the canoe with measured, even strokes, pulling upstream. It became increasingly evident that she was taking me to a specific place. I still could not see very well in the distance because of the bleak, grey mist. Dead grass like old beards hung into the water, and I could see dark and shadowless roots in countless shapes and sizes. There were clumps of horsetail and we canoed through water lilies close enough to reach and touch marshgrass on the shore. Then we cut around a bend and something gleamed faintly ahead. The mist was too dense to see through for a moment and then, as we glided into the sunlight again, I saw a line of fifteen canoes on a stretch of beach. We paddled quickly. Fog completely covered the trees on shore as we pulled in between the other beached canoes. We dragged the craft forward and turned it over.

"What are all these canoes?" I asked.

"They belong to hunters," Agnes said.

"We don't want to have a picnic around a bunch of hunters."

"These are special hunters," Agnes said.

I was now following her down a path along the bank of the river. Agnes cut to the right and I could see only her vague outline in the mist. We were in a forest of quaking aspens. She reached back and took my hand and pulled me along behind her. The further we walked, the more dense the brush and brambles became. Visability was next to nothing.

We emerged from the bushes into a vast, fog-laden clearing. Over the top of the billowing mist I thought I saw several shields sitting on large tripods. The sight was exalting, and I stood in a trancelike state wondering if I had really seen them or if my mind was playing tricks on me. By now the quickening fog had enveloped everything.

"Was that a mirage?" I asked.

Agnes took my hand again and we walked straight into the bank of fog; stepping gingerly in the wet grass. My clothes were damp from dew. I couldn't see a thing; even Agnes was barely discernible next to me. The fog appeared to be a pearl grey substance, and

202 : SHIELD-MADE-OF-SHADOWS

every once in a while light stabbed through it, turning it to a milky brilliance.

"Here," she suddenly said. "Stand here and look up and tell me what you see."

As if dawn were breaking, the barriers of fog parted on a beam of light. I saw a clearing before us and out of the silence and immobility of the fog an orchestration of brightly colored medicine shields stood like golden suns flashing brilliantly in the intense daylight. I counted them. There were forty-four, an overwhelming number.

"Look carefully at each shield," Agnes said, watching my reaction intently.

Now I understood I was standing in a ring of shields. They were of wondrous painted designs in all colors of yellow, muddy red, white, brown, pale blue, turquoise, and jet black, some with silver-and-black-pointed feathers or hawk, eagle, and owl feathers flapping in the breeze. They were marvelously exquisite with woven beads, fur, and fringes. The pole I was standing in front of held my own north shield.

Apprehension mixed with joy caused me to tremble. Where had my shield come from and what were all these others? It was then that I saw my shield was flanked on both sides by Agnes's left-hand shield and Ruby's Spirit-of-the-Deer shield. I tried to remember everything that Agnes had told me about a sisterhood of the shields. I recalled that Red Dog had said no such thing existed. What about the sky shields? With that thought I really became confused.

"I don't understand."

Just then a sudden strong wind came up, pressing the fog downward, then chasing it away. Behind the tripods I saw a huge log and rock structure that looked like a hunting lodge. I couldn't imagine why it was out here in the middle of nowhere. When I turned around I was even more shocked. Agnes was standing on my right in front of the tripod that held her shield. Ruby was standing on my left. There were forty-one other women in the circle in front of their shields. They were of varying ages, mostly over fifty. Not all of them were Indian. All attention seemed to focus on me. I didn't know what to say, or what was required, or even why I had been brought here.

My heart was pounding. All at once the oldest Indian woman I had ever seen, with long white braids and wearing a mauve dress and a fringed shawl, stepped out into the center of the circle. She said, "My name is Grace Walking Stick. We welcome you." She looked directly into my eyes; and I looked into hers. It was like staring into the desert. "Do you remember who you are?" she asked.

"Yes," I answered.

"Then look carefully at each one of us."

I looked at every woman there, and with tears of inexplicable joy I realized that something within me recognized each and every woman. I also saw the reincarnation of women's lonely dream upon the earth. With this came the terrible strain of knowledge, and I saw the irrevocable consequences of action. Into this vision I was drawn—into this mysterious joy of being, this mirror of the joyous and brutal facts of life and death, pain and pleasure. My mind followed a labyrinth of symbols, images, and primeval ideas, each somehow more fascinating than the last, yet behind each a terrible, aching loneliness. How few people ever surrender to a feeling of love, know it, breathe it. And now out of that dark, karmic wheel, a bridge was being formed. I knew from that moment forward I would always know my kinship with these women.

"There is one rule," Grace said. "You must never disclose the identities of any of us to anyone."

I said that I understood. I was surprised that I knew many of them already. Each of them was special. What I saw in their faces was completeness. Each of them was a realized and loving woman, an enlightened woman. They were my sisterhood. I had found my circle.